100 AMAZING FACTS ABOUT SPACE

Contents

"Look up at the stars and not down at your feet. Try to make sense of what you see, and wonder about what makes the universe exist. Be curious."

—*Stephen Hawking*

Introduction

Welcome, dear reader, to an extraordinary journey that will take you to the edges of the universe and back. Prepare to embark on a cosmic adventure as you delve into "1000 Amazing Facts about Space," where every page unravels a new mystery, a new wonder, a new spectacle of the celestial world.

Space: an endless expanse of time and cosmos, a tapestry of stars and galaxies, black holes and nebulas, planets and moons. It is here that stars are born and die, galaxies collide, and beautiful nebulae house stellar nurseries. It is the frontier of human exploration, a subject of eternal intrigue and enduring curiosity.

In this book, we aim to answer some of the questions that have fascinated mankind for centuries. What does the surface of Mars look like? What lies beyond the edges of our universe? How does a black hole form, and what would you experience if you fell into one? These and many more fascinating facts about the universe and our place within it await your discovery.

"1000 Amazing Facts about Space" invites you to marvel at the complexities of our universe. From the unimaginably massive galaxies to the infinitesimally small particles, from the brightest supernovae to the darkest corners of the universe, from our intimate celestial neighborhood to the most distant corners of the observable cosmos, we've compiled the most intriguing, the most astonishing, and the most thought-provoking facts about the universe.

So prepare yourself for a journey through space and time, as we unravel the mysteries of the cosmos, one amazing fact at a time. Hold on tight, your journey through the stars begins now!

Fact 1 - The Roaring Sun: A Symphony in Space

Hey there, space explorer! Have you ever thought about the Sun as a huge, glowing concert happening right in our neighborhood of the universe? Welcome to the symphony of our very own star - the Sun.

The Sun, unlike the Earth, doesn't have a solid surface. Instead, it's a giant ball of glowing gases, making a wonderful cosmic music. This is thanks to a process called 'helioseismology' where the surface of the Sun oscillates, creating sound waves that ripple across the star, like the surface of a drum.

These oscillations make the Sun 'ring' like a bell, creating a symphony that sadly, we can't hear directly as sound cannot travel through the vacuum of space. But don't worry! Scientists have developed special techniques to 'listen' to this solar symphony, helping them to understand more about the Sun's composition and dynamics.

So, next time you're basking in the warm sunlight, remember - you're experiencing the result of a spectacular cosmic concert that's been playing for over 4.5 billion years. Isn't that an incredible fact about our roaring Sun?

Fact 2 - Star-Studded Tales: How Stars are Born and Die

Are you ready for a stellar journey, young astronomer? Let's dive into the life of stars, witnessing their birth and understanding their eventual fate. You're about to discover the exciting life cycle of stars!

Stars are born in gigantic clouds of dust and gas in space known as 'nebulae'. As gravity pulls the dust and gas together, the dense 'core' begins to heat up - forming a 'protostar'. With time, the heat and pressure in the core become so intense that nuclear reactions begin, and ta-da - a star is born!

But stars aren't eternal. When they exhaust their nuclear fuel, they die in spectacular ways based on their mass. A smaller star like our Sun ends its life as a 'white dwarf', quietly fading into the cosmic backdrop. However, a massive star explodes violently in a 'supernova', sometimes leaving behind an exotic 'neutron star' or a 'black hole'.

From humble beginnings in cosmic nurseries to grand finales that can outshine galaxies, stars lead remarkable lives. Isn't the universe and its star-studded tales simply fascinating?

Fact 3 - Galaxy on a Diet: Dark Matter Mystery

Howdy, young cosmic detective! Are you ready to explore one of the greatest mysteries of our universe? Brace yourself as we delve into the enigma of dark matter.

Let's start by blowing your mind - did you know that about 85% of the matter in the universe is invisible? Yes, you read that right! It's called 'dark matter' and it doesn't interact with light or any other electromagnetic waves, making it extremely hard to detect.

Why do we believe in something we can't see? Well, when scientists looked at how galaxies spin, they found something puzzling. Galaxies rotate so fast that they should tear themselves apart, but they don't. It seems as though something unseen, a.k.a dark matter, is adding extra 'gravitational glue' to hold galaxies together.

Though we can't 'see' dark matter, its gravitational pull reveals its presence, playing a vital role in shaping our universe. Unraveling the dark matter mystery is like a thrilling cosmic detective story, and who knows, maybe you could be the one to solve it in the future! Isn't that an amazing challenge?

Fact 4 - The Curious Case of Time Dilation

Ready for a mind-bending adventure, time traveler? Today, we'll explore the fascinating concept of time dilation. Time travel may not be just for science fiction after all!

Imagine you're on a spaceship traveling close to the speed of light while your friend stays back on Earth. Did you know that time would pass differently for you both? This is time dilation - a prediction of Einstein's Theory of Relativity.

As you zoom around in your high-speed spaceship, time would 'slow down' for you relative to your friend on Earth. If you spent a few years in space and then returned, you'd find your Earth-bound friend would have aged more than you. You would have traveled into the future!

Sounds like something straight out of a sci-fi movie, doesn't it? But it's real! Scientists have tested and confirmed time dilation with super precise atomic clocks. So, time dilation is our universe's own version of a time machine. Isn't that an amazing trip?

Fact 5 - How Fast Does Earth Travel?

Buckle up, adventurer! Ever wondered how fast you're zooming through space while you're just sitting and reading this? Prepare to be amazed by our cosmic speedometer: Earth's astonishing speed!

Earth rotates on its axis, which gives us day and night. At the equator, the Earth's rotation speed is about 1,670 kilometers per hour (around 1,040 miles per hour). That's faster than the speed of sound!

However, Earth doesn't only spin on its axis, it also orbits around the Sun at an average speed of about 107,000 kilometers per hour (or 66,500 miles per hour). That's about 30 kilometers every second - over 50 times faster than a bullet!

But hold on, there's more! Our entire Solar System is moving around the center of the Milky Way Galaxy at a mind-boggling speed of approximately 828,000 kilometers per hour (515,000 miles per hour). So, no matter how still you think you are, you're always on a cosmic joyride. Isn't that an awesome thought?

Fact 6 - Zipping Around: Speed of Light Fun Facts

Hello, speedster! Are you ready to break all the speed records? Get set as we unravel some fun facts about the ultimate speed limit in the universe - the speed of light!

Light, as you know, is very fast. But did you know just how fast? Brace yourself - the speed of light is a staggering 299,792 kilometers per second (or about 186,282 miles per second). It's the fastest speed at which information or matter can travel.

To give you an idea, if you could travel at the speed of light, you could zip around the Earth about 7.5 times in just one second! Or travel to the Moon and back in under 3 seconds. Talk about a quick trip!

This unimaginable speed also helps astronomers study the universe. When they say a star is a million light years away, it means the light we're seeing from that star started its journey a million years ago. So looking at stars is like time-traveling into the past! Isn't the speed of light just mind-blowing?

Fact 7 - The Beauty of Gravitational Lensing

Hello, cosmic artist! Are you ready to witness a marvelous light show painted by the universe itself? Welcome to the incredible phenomenon of gravitational lensing!

Gravity is a powerful force. It's so powerful that it can even bend light! When the light from a distant object, like a galaxy, passes by a massive object, such as another galaxy, the gravity of the massive object can warp and deflect the light. This is known as 'gravitational lensing'.

What does this look like? Picture a cosmic mirage. Light bent by gravitational lensing can form arcs, streaks, or even multiple images of the distant object. Sometimes, if perfectly aligned, it can create a stunning 'Einstein Ring', named after Albert Einstein who predicted this effect.

Gravitational lensing is not just beautiful, it's useful too! It allows astronomers to study distant galaxies that would otherwise be too faint to see and even detect invisible dark matter. Isn't it amazing how gravity can paint such mesmerizing rainbows in space?

Fact 8 - The Little Star That Could: The Mighty Neutron Star

Hello, star gazer! Are you ready to meet one of the universe's ultimate champions? Get ready to uncover the amazing power of the little but mighty neutron star!

Neutron stars are the remnants of massive stars that have gone supernova. They're incredibly dense - so dense that just a sugar-cube-sized amount of neutron star material would weigh about a billion tons on Earth. That's roughly the weight of Mount Everest!

These tiny titans, only about 20 kilometers (12 miles) across, spin incredibly fast, some as fast as 600 times per second! They also have the strongest magnetic fields known in the universe, about a trillion times stronger than Earth's magnetic field.

These amazing characteristics make neutron stars unique cosmic laboratories. Studying them helps scientists understand matter under extreme conditions that can't be recreated in any Earth-based lab. From their tiny size to their mighty nature, neutron stars truly show us that size isn't everything. Isn't the universe just full of surprises?

Fact 9 - A Moon with Rivers and Lakes

Greetings, space explorer! Ready for a journey to one of the most intriguing places in our solar system? Let's visit Titan, Saturn's largest moon and a world that remarkably resembles Earth.

Titan is the only moon in our solar system with a dense atmosphere and the only other place besides Earth where stable liquids exist on the surface. But instead of water, these are lakes and rivers of liquid methane and ethane, which exist as gases on Earth!

The weather on Titan also seems like a chilly version of home. It has a methane cycle similar to Earth's water cycle, with methane rain falling from the clouds, filling lakes and rivers, and evaporating back into the atmosphere.

Despite the extreme cold (temperatures can plunge to minus 290 degrees Fahrenheit), Titan's similarity to Earth makes it a prime target in the search for life beyond our planet. A moon with rivers and lakes - isn't that a captivating thought? The universe never ceases to surprise us, does it?

Fact 10 - The Persevering Rovers: Rolling Robots on Mars

Hello, future Martian! Have you ever dreamt of rolling around Mars, exploring its red terrain? Let's get to know our robotic ambassadors who've been doing just that: the Mars rovers!

The Mars rovers are an impressive bunch of robots, built to explore the surface of Mars. They're designed to withstand extreme temperatures, navigate rocky terrain, and carry out scientific missions. They've been helping us uncover the secrets of the Red Planet, right from its ancient wet past to the possibility of it having once hosted life.

The most recent rover, Perseverance, even carried a small helicopter, Ingenuity, marking the first attempt at powered flight on another planet. This innovative duo continues to make groundbreaking discoveries and pave the way for future human exploration.

From the golf-cart-sized Spirit and Opportunity, to the car-sized Curiosity and Perseverance, these roving robots have been the eyes and ears of scientists on Mars. They've made Mars feel a little bit closer to us, don't you think? They are true space heroes - persevering against all odds!

Fact 11 - The Ultimate Long-Distance Call

Hello, future astronaut! Ever wondered how we communicate with our spacecraft zipping around in space? Let's talk about the ultimate long-distance call - reaching out to our spaceships.

You might be thinking we just pick up a space phone and dial the spacecraft. However, it's a little more complex than that. We use a network of large antennas around Earth, called the Deep Space Network (DSN), to send and receive messages to our spacecraft.

But it's not an instant chat. If we send a message from Earth to a spacecraft near Mars, it can take about 20 minutes for the message to reach, and then another 20 minutes for the reply to get back to Earth. That's a 40-minute round trip for your message!

This communication delay is something future Mars astronauts will have to contend with. Imagine waiting 40 minutes to get a response to your text! It's yet another amazing challenge of space exploration. Isn't it fascinating how we've learned to make these ultimate long-distance calls?

Fact 12 - Why Does the Moon Change Shape?

Hello, lunar observer! Ever wondered why the moon changes its shape in the sky? From a thin crescent to a bright full disk - let's explore this fascinating lunar dance.

Contrary to what it may seem, the moon isn't changing its shape. What's actually happening is that we're seeing different amounts of the moon's surface lit by the Sun as the moon orbits around the Earth. This creates the moon's phases.

The new moon phase happens when the moon is between the Earth and the Sun, and its illuminated side is facing away from us. As it orbits around the Earth, more and more of its sunlit side becomes visible, leading to a crescent, then a half moon, and finally a full moon.

The full moon happens when the moon is on the opposite side of the Earth from the Sun, and we can see its entire illuminated side. As it continues to orbit, less and less of the lit side is visible, and the moon wanes back to a new moon. The moon's changing shape is just a beautiful cosmic dance between the Sun, the Moon, and the Earth. Doesn't that make you appreciate our night sky even more?

Fact 13 - Dancing Universes: The Theory of Multiverse

Hello, cosmic thinker! Ready to dive into one of the most intriguing ideas in modern physics? Let's explore the mind-boggling theory of the multiverse.

Imagine this: what if our universe, with all its galaxies and stars, planets and moons, was not the only universe? What if there were an infinite number of other universes, each with its own laws of physics, stars, and possibly life forms? That's the concept of the multiverse.

This isn't just a wild idea. It arises from quantum mechanics and the theory of cosmic inflation. In some versions of these theories, our universe could be one bubble in an infinite cosmic foam of bubble universes. Other theories suggest that there could be parallel universes existing alongside our own!

While the multiverse theory is still just that - a theory - and has yet to be proven, it's a fascinating concept that tickles our imagination. The possibility of multiple, even infinite, universes makes our cosmic dance even more awe-inspiring, don't you think? It's just another example of the astonishing ideas space science presents us.

Fact 14 - Sibling Rivalry: Jupiter, The Largest Planet

Hello, planetary explorer! Ready to meet the big brother of our solar family? Let's get acquainted with Jupiter, the largest planet in our solar system.

Jupiter is so massive that it weighs more than twice as much as all the other planets in the solar system combined! If Jupiter were hollow, you could fit more than 1,300 Earths inside it. Now, that's a hefty planet!

Don't be fooled by its size, Jupiter is also a fast spinner. Despite its mammoth size, it has the shortest day of all the planets, spinning around once every 9.9 hours. Its fast rotation causes the planet to slightly flatten, making it wider at its equator.

Jupiter's vast size also gives it a powerful gravitational pull, which influences many asteroids and has captured a whopping 79 moons at the last count. So, when it comes to the solar system's sibling rivalry, Jupiter clearly takes the crown. Doesn't knowing this make you marvel at the diversity of our solar system?

Fact 15 - Space is a Vacuum, but It's Not Empty!

Hey there, space detective! Ready to bust a myth? You've probably heard that space is a vacuum, but did you know it's not entirely empty? Let's dig into this cosmic mystery.

When we say space is a vacuum, we mean it's void of air and matter like we're used to on Earth. However, it's not completely devoid of stuff. Across the universe, there are tiny particles scattered about, remnants of ancient stars and galaxies.

Even the emptiest parts of space contain a few hydrogen atoms per cubic meter. In denser regions, like nebulae where new stars are born, there are thousands to millions of atoms in the same space. And let's not forget about cosmic rays, particles moving near light speed, that constantly zip through the cosmos.

Even photons, the particles of light, fill space with their invisible presence. So next time you look up at the night sky, remember, space isn't as empty as it seems. Isn't it amazing to think about what's really out there in the vast 'emptiness'?

Fact 16 - How Your Body Contains Stardust

Hello, stardust being! Have you ever thought about what you're made of? Let's reveal a fantastic fact: your body contains stardust!

That's right. The carbon, nitrogen, and oxygen atoms in our bodies, as well as atoms of all other heavy elements, were created in previous generations of stars over 4.5 billion years ago. As these stars died, they expelled these elements out into space.

These atoms then mingled with other material and eventually formed a new star system, with planets - including Earth. The atoms in your body are from those stars. They're billions of years old and have traveled across the cosmos to become you!

You are literally made of stardust. Every time you breathe, you're using oxygen that was once part of a star! Isn't that an awe-inspiring thought? You and I, and everything we see around us, are part of this amazing cosmic recycling story. Makes you feel quite connected to the universe, doesn't it?

Fact 17 - Your Weight in Space

Hello, space adventurer! Ever wondered how much you'd weigh on other planets? Let's take a cosmic journey and step on the scale in space.

Your weight isn't the same everywhere. It depends on the amount of gravity pulling on you, which changes from planet to planet. On Earth, if you weigh 100 pounds, you're not going to weigh the same on Jupiter or Mars.

On Mars, for instance, you'd weigh only about 38% of your Earth weight because Mars is smaller and has less gravity. So, if you weigh 100 pounds on Earth, you'd be a light 38 pounds on Mars!

On the other hand, Jupiter, being the most massive planet in our solar system, has a strong gravitational pull. If you weigh 100 pounds on Earth, you'd weigh a whopping 236 pounds on Jupiter. Now, that's a heavy thought!

Isn't it fun to imagine stepping on a scale on other planets? It's just another example of how different and exciting the universe can be. Space travel could literally be a weighty issue!

Fact 18 - Diamonds in the Sky: The Wealth of Saturn's Rings

Hello, cosmic treasure hunter! Have you ever wanted to find diamonds in the sky? Let's discover the wealth hidden in Saturn's rings.

Saturn, the jewel of our solar system, is well known for its beautiful rings. But did you know that those rings could be filled with diamonds? That's right, diamonds could be raining down on Saturn as we speak!

Here's how it works. Saturn's atmosphere is rich in methane, and when lightning storms turn methane into soot, the pressure and temperature conditions could transform that soot into graphite and then into diamonds as it falls towards the planet.

These diamonds wouldn't last forever, though. As they fall deeper into the planet, the extreme heat and pressure would melt them into a liquid sea. Still, it's a dazzling thought, isn't it?

Can you imagine a diamond rain? Saturn truly is a jewel in more ways than one. It's just another mind-blowing aspect of our amazing universe. The cosmic treasure chest is full of surprises, isn't it?

Fact 19 - The Fastest Things in the Universe

Hello, cosmic racer! Have you ever wondered what the fastest things in the universe are? Let's explore these cosmic speedsters.

At the top of the speed list is light, zooming along at a mind-boggling speed of about 186,282 miles per second (299,792 kilometers per second). Nothing in the universe can travel faster than light!

But what about matter? Well, particles called high-energy cosmic rays can reach 99.9999% the speed of light. These tiny particles, from sources like supernovas or black holes, are the universe's natural speedsters!

In terms of larger objects, pulsars - incredibly dense, rapidly rotating stars - can spin dozens of times per second. Their speed can reach up to 70,000 kilometers per second at the surface!

Isn't it incredible how fast things can go in the universe? It gives a new meaning to the word 'speed', doesn't it? The cosmos is full of thrilling races, each more surprising than the last. How's that for a space race?

Fact 20 - Astronaut's Menu: Eating in Outer Space

Hello, space foodie! Have you ever wondered what it's like to eat in space? Let's explore the astronaut's unique menu.

In space, there's no refrigerator or microwave to store or heat food. That's why most of the food for astronauts is freeze-dried, dehydrated, or thermally stabilized. Before eating, astronauts add water to their meals, which they get from a dispenser on their spacecraft.

Just like on Earth, astronauts eat a variety of foods like vegetables, fruit, nuts, chicken, beef, seafood, and desserts. But instead of being fresh, they're packaged in vacuum-sealed pouches. Even drinks come in powdered form!

Eating in space can be a fun challenge. Because there's no gravity, food particles can float around, so astronauts have to eat carefully to avoid making a mess. They often use tortillas instead of bread to avoid crumbs floating everywhere!

Imagine having dinner while floating in space, looking at the Earth below. The astronaut's menu might be different, but the view certainly makes up for it! Isn't it fascinating how even ordinary things like eating can be so different in space?

Fact 21 - Black Hole's Dinner Time: The Event Horizon

Hello, cosmic explorer! Have you ever wondered what happens at a black hole's dinner time? Let's uncover the mystery of the event horizon.

A black hole is an area in space where gravity is so strong that nothing, not even light, can escape its grasp. The boundary around a black hole where the escape speed equals the speed of light is called the event horizon.

Once something crosses the event horizon, it's officially dinner time for the black hole. Everything, from dust particles to stars, can be devoured if they get too close. This process is known as accretion.

From outside the event horizon, it seems like time stops. That's because the immense gravity of a black hole distorts time and space. Anything falling in seems to slow down and fade away, never actually seen crossing the horizon.

How's that for a cosmic meal? The event horizon is a point of no return, the ultimate boundary in the universe. It's just another reminder of how incredibly wild and amazing our universe is, wouldn't you say?

Fact 22 - Galactic Monsters: The Size of the Milky Way

Hello, star traveler! Ever wondered how big our galaxy is? Let's journey across the galactic monster that is the Milky Way.

Our galaxy, the Milky Way, is a grand cosmic island that houses hundreds of billions of stars, including our own Sun. But just how big is it? Brace yourself: it's about 100,000 light-years in diameter!

A light-year, as you know, is the distance light travels in a year, and that's about 5.9 trillion miles (9.5 trillion kilometers)! So, multiply that by 100,000 and you start to get an idea of the enormous size of our galaxy.

In terms of thickness, the Milky Way isn't very chunky. It's about 1,000 light-years thick, making it 100 times longer than it is thick. Imagine a pancake, and you'll get a rough idea of our galaxy's shape!

Isn't it amazing to live in such a vast, pancake-shaped galaxy? And to think, the Milky Way is just one of billions of galaxies in the universe! It's a big cosmic world out there, isn't it?

Fact 23 - From Sunrise to Sunset: A Day on Venus

Hello, planet hopper! Have you ever wondered what a day is like on Venus? Let's experience a sunrise to sunset on our neighboring planet.

A "day" on any planet is the time it takes for it to rotate once on its axis. On Earth, that's 24 hours. But on Venus, things are a bit more leisurely. A Venusian day is about 243 Earth days long. That's right, over eight months for one rotation!

Moreover, Venus has a peculiar twist. It rotates in the opposite direction of most other planets, including Earth. This means on Venus, the Sun rises in the west and sets in the east. How's that for topsy-turvy?

And hold on, because here's another odd fact: Venus' year, the time it takes to orbit the Sun, is shorter than its day, about 225 Earth days. So, on Venus, a day is longer than a year!

Isn't Venus' day fascinating? It's a perfect example of how diverse and unexpected our solar system can be. A day on Venus is truly like no other day!

Fact 24 - Comets: The Cosmic Snowballs of the Universe

Hello, space enthusiast! Do you love a good snowball fight? Let's dive into the universe's take on snowballs: comets!

Comets are often called the cosmic snowballs of the universe. They're made of ice, rock, dust, and organic compounds. When far from the Sun, they are quiet and serene, just like a snowball in your hand.

As a comet gets closer to the Sun, though, it heats up and things start to change. The heat makes the ices in the comet vaporize, creating a glowing head and a tail that points away from the Sun due to the solar wind. The sight of this can be breathtaking!

Some comets take thousands of years to orbit the Sun, while others take just a few years. The most famous, Halley's Comet, swings by Earth every 76 years. Its next visit will be in 2061, so start your countdown!

How's that for a snowball fight? Comets are not just amazing to look at, they're also vital to understanding more about our solar system and the early universe. Watch the skies, you never know when the next one will show up!

Fact 25 - Red Planet Mysteries: Life on Mars?

Hello, Mars explorer! Are you ready to uncover one of the most thrilling questions in the universe: Is there life on Mars?

Mars, our red neighbor, has been the subject of fascination for centuries, especially when it comes to the possibility of life. In the past, people thought they saw canals and vegetation on Mars, sparking ideas of Martian civilizations.

While we haven't found any Martians yet, the discovery of water ice on Mars has kept the hope of life alive. If life exists as we know it, water is essential, and Mars has it! It's just frozen in the polar ice caps and beneath the surface.

Rovers like Perseverance are searching for signs of ancient microbial life. They're examining rocks, drilling for samples, and exploring the terrain for clues. Could there have been tiny life forms on Mars billions of years ago?

What do you think, explorer? Could there have been life on Mars in the past? Or could there be life on Mars right now, hiding just out of sight? The question is still open, and maybe you'll be part of the generation to find out!

Fact 26 - Polar Opposites: The Magnetic Field of Earth

Hello, magnetic maven! Ever used a compass and wondered how it works? It's all thanks to the amazing magnetic field of the Earth. Let's explore!

Our planet isn't just a big ball of rock and water; it's also a giant magnet. Deep within Earth's core, hot liquid iron creates a magnetic field that reaches out into space. This invisible shield has north and south poles, just like a bar magnet.

This magnetic field is crucial for life. It protects us from harmful solar radiation, which can damage life and technologies. When charged particles from the Sun collide with the magnetic field, it creates the stunning natural light displays called auroras.

Sometimes the magnetic field flips, switching the North and South Poles. Don't worry, this happens over thousands of years, and the last switch was about 780,000 years ago. Scientists are still figuring out why and how these flips occur.

Isn't our Earth incredible? Not only does it provide us with everything we need to live, but it also invisibly shields us every day. How cool is that? The Earth truly is a marvel of the cosmos!

Fact 27 - Pluto's Heart: Love From The Edge of Solar System

Hello, cosmic adventurer! Do you have a soft spot for the underdog? Let's journey to the edge of our solar system and explore the enduring charm of Pluto.

Pluto, once considered the ninth planet, now a dwarf planet, captured hearts worldwide when the New Horizons spacecraft sent back images in 2015. What caught everyone's eye? A giant heart-shaped feature on its surface, now named Tombaugh Regio, after Pluto's discoverer.

This heart isn't beating, but it's full of surprises. The left side, named Sputnik Planitia, is a vast plain of nitrogen ice. Its surface is divided into polygonal cells, believed to be shaped by slow thermal convection.

On the right side, you'll find rugged highlands and deep pits. Researchers believe these features tell a tale of a violent past, possibly including impacts and cryovolcanism - that's ice volcanoes!

Isn't that a captivating image of Pluto - a planet marked by an icy heart and a fascinating geological history? It's a constant reminder that even at the edge of our solar system, there are wonders that can touch our hearts, inspire us, and drive us to keep exploring.

Fact 28 - Spinning Stars: The Lighthouse Effect of Pulsars

Hello, stargazer! Have you ever seen a lighthouse on a dark night? Now imagine one in the deep sea of the cosmos - welcome to the world of pulsars!

Pulsars are neutron stars, the leftovers of massive stars that have exploded as supernovae. But these aren't just any old space leftovers; they spin incredibly fast and have strong magnetic fields, producing beams of radiation from their poles.

Just like a lighthouse, these beams sweep across the universe as the pulsar rotates. If Earth is in the path of the beam, we see a flash of light or a pulse every time the pulsar spins around, hence the name 'pulsar'.

Some pulsars spin several hundred times per second! Their precise timing rivals even the best atomic clocks on Earth. Astronomers use them to test the limits of physics, including the theory of general relativity.

So, stargazer, next time you look up at the night sky, remember that among those twinkling stars, there are cosmic lighthouses spinning and beaming across the vast cosmic sea. Isn't the universe filled with the most spectacular wonders?

Fact 29 - Shower of Stars: The Spectacular Meteor Showers

Hey there, shooting star spotter! Have you ever made a wish upon a falling star? Let's dive into the breathtaking phenomenon known as meteor showers.

Meteor showers happen when Earth passes through the trail of dust and small rocks left by a comet or asteroid. As these bits of cosmic debris enter Earth's atmosphere, they burn up and create a streak of light. That's what we call a shooting star!

The most amazing part is when many of these "shooting stars" appear in the sky in a short amount of time, creating a "meteor shower". Some meteor showers, like the Perseids or the Geminids, can feature over 100 meteors per hour!

Despite their name, these "shooting stars" aren't stars at all, but tiny bits of space dust burning up high in our atmosphere. Yet their beauty has inspired countless people over the centuries.

So, next time there's a meteor shower, why not gather some friends for a nighttime picnic? Just lie back and watch the spectacular show in the sky. Don't forget to make a wish!

Fact 30 - Earth's Mirror: The Discovery of Exoplanets

Greetings, fellow space explorer! Have you ever wondered if there's another Earth out there? Let's venture into the realm of exoplanets, planets that orbit stars outside of our solar system.

The discovery of exoplanets has reshaped our understanding of the cosmos. As of now, thousands of these alien worlds have been found, some of them even in the habitable zone of their stars, where conditions might just be right for life.

How do we find these distant worlds? One way is the "transit method". When a planet passes in front of its star, it dims the star's light slightly. By observing these tiny dips in brightness, scientists can infer the presence of an exoplanet.

Some exoplanets discovered are super-Earths, bigger than Earth but smaller than Neptune. Some are gas giants like Jupiter, and some, excitingly, are even Earth-sized in the habitable zone. While we've yet to find a perfect Earth twin, the search continues.

So, next time you look up at the stars, consider this: around one of them, there might just be a planet like our own, waiting to be discovered. Isn't that a thrilling thought?

Fact 31 - The Invisible Pull: Understanding Gravity

Hello, my curious friend! Have you ever wondered why you stay firmly on the ground instead of floating away? It's all thanks to a force we cannot see but experience every day - gravity!

Gravity is the force that attracts two objects towards each other. Every object that has mass also has gravity. The more massive an object is, the stronger its gravitational pull. That's why we stick to the large Earth instead of Earth sticking to us!

But gravity isn't just an Earth thing. It's a universal force that's at play across the entire cosmos. It's what keeps the Moon in orbit around Earth and our planet in orbit around the Sun. Gravity also forms stars, galaxies, and the structure of the Universe itself.

So next time you jump up and come back down, remember you're experiencing a fundamental force that shapes the cosmos. From the leap of a frog to the orbits of distant galaxies, gravity is the silent director of the cosmic ballet. Isn't it amazing to be part of this grand dance?

Fact 32 - Alien Skies: Color of the Sky on Other Planets

Hey, my rainbow chaser! Have you ever wondered what color the sky is on other planets? Let's take an imaginary tour across the solar system and discover the unique sky hues of alien worlds.

Starting with our neighbor, Mars, you'd witness a peachy-pink sky during the day, which turns to cool blue at sunset - the exact opposite of Earth! This color flip happens because of the way the thin Martian atmosphere scatters sunlight.

What about gas giants like Jupiter and Saturn? Since they lack a solid surface, defining 'sky' is tricky. But if you were hovering in their upper atmospheres, you'd see a pale yellow sky thanks to the abundance of ammonia clouds.

And on Titan, Saturn's largest moon, the thick orange haze of the atmosphere would give the sky an eerie, golden glow. On Venus, you would be surrounded by a golden sky filled with thick sulfuric clouds, while on Neptune, methane in the atmosphere would give the sky a deep blue color.

Isn't it fascinating how diverse our solar system is? While we have a blue sky above us on Earth, remember that out there, there's a whole spectrum of alien skies waiting to be explored!

Fact 33 - The Cosmic Microwave Background

Hello, my little time traveler! How would you like to take a glimpse at the Universe's baby picture? Yes, you heard right - we can actually see what the Universe looked like when it was just a cosmic toddler, thanks to something called the Cosmic Microwave Background, or CMB.

The CMB is a faint glow of radiation that fills all of space. It's the oldest light we can see, created just 380,000 years after the Big Bang. Back then, the Universe was a hot, dense soup of particles. As it expanded and cooled, light was finally able to travel freely, creating the CMB.

This cosmic snapshot reveals lots about our Universe's early days. Tiny fluctuations in the CMB's temperature tell us how matter was distributed back then, which helps us understand how galaxies formed. It even supports the idea of cosmic inflation - a theory that the Universe expanded super quickly just after the Big Bang.

So, you see, looking at the CMB is like opening a baby album of the Universe. It's our best evidence for the Big Bang and a key tool for understanding the cosmos. Pretty cool, isn't it?

Fact 34 - Catch a Falling Star: What is a Meteorite?

Hey, stargazer! Have you ever seen a shooting star and made a wish? Those 'stars' are actually tiny bits of rock or metal called meteoroids. When one of these soars through our atmosphere and survives to reach the ground, we call it a meteorite.

Now, imagine you're watching the night sky and you spot a streak of light. That's a meteor or a "shooting star". The light you see isn't the meteoroid itself, but the glowing hot air as the meteoroid speeds through Earth's atmosphere.

If that meteoroid is big enough and doesn't completely burn up, it might make it to the ground as a meteorite. These space rocks give us precious insights about our solar system. Some are pieces of asteroids or possibly even other planets, and others are as old as the solar system itself.

So, remember, the next time you see a "shooting star," you're actually seeing a tiny bit of the cosmos visiting Earth. Who knows, maybe you could even find a piece of it in your backyard!

Fact 35 - Under the Gas Giant's Clouds

Hey, weather watcher! Think we have wild weather here on Earth? Hold on to your umbrella because the gas giant Jupiter has us beat. Its atmosphere is one massive, swirling stormy chaos, and it's unlike anything we have here on our home planet.

You've probably seen pictures of Jupiter's Great Red Spot, right? That's a storm that's been going for at least 300 years! It's so huge that you could fit three Earths inside it. Imagine seeing that on your weather forecast!

But that's not the only storm on Jupiter. The entire planet is covered in bands of clouds, all whirling around in different directions. These are made from ammonia and water, and the various colors come from different types of cloud particles, as well as effects of sunlight.

Next time you're caught in a rain shower, remember - it could be worse. You could be on Jupiter, where the storms are bigger, badder, and have been blowing for centuries! Wouldn't that be a sight to see?

Fact 36 - The Planet with Double Sunrise

Hello, my adventurous friend! Ever fancy a double sunrise? If yes, then the planet Mercury is the vacation spot for you! But remember, you'll need your most durable space suit - it's seriously hot out there!

Mercury, the tiny powerhouse nearest to the Sun, has a strange, slow spin. It turns so sluggishly that if you were standing on its surface, you'd see the Sun rise, stop in the sky, backtrack a bit, and then rise again before it sets. How's that for a morning show?

It happens due to a weird phenomenon called 'retrograde motion'. Mercury's day is so long (it takes 59 Earth days for it to spin once on its axis), and its year is so short (88 Earth days), that from a certain spot on the surface, the Sun appears to move backward in the sky.

So, pack your sunblock and strap in for a double sunrise, space traveler! Just remember that a Mercury day is super long. By the time the Sun sets, you'll be older by a couple of Earth months!

Fact 37 - Our Ever-Expanding Universe: The Big Bang Theory

Imagine this: all the stars, galaxies, and space as you know it, starting from a single point and then - BOOM! - it's everywhere. You've just pictured the Big Bang Theory, the concept of how our Universe was born!

About 13.8 billion years ago, the Universe was an extremely hot, dense point nearly infinitely small. Then, it rapidly inflated, expanded, and cooled, eventually leading to the formation of atoms, stars, and galaxies. This is the simplified story of the Big Bang.

This isn't just a fun theory; we have evidence! Cosmic microwave background radiation, which is a faint glow that fills the entire Universe, is the cooled remnant from that intense, hot early stage. It's like the Universe's baby photo, giving us a glimpse of its origin.

So, next time you look up at the night sky, remember: those twinkling stars are all part of an immense cosmic arena that started as a tiny, hot, dense spot. Who knew something so colossal could come from something so small? The Universe truly is the greatest magic show!

Fact 38 - The Telescopic Revolution

Picture yourself peering into a tube, one eye squeezed shut, the other gazing at the starlit heavens. You're standing in the shoes of a man named Galileo Galilei, who way back in 1609, dramatically transformed how we understand the Universe.

Galileo didn't invent the telescope - it was the Dutch. But he was the first person to aim one towards the sky, turning our world upside down. He saw the craters of the Moon, the phases of Venus, and Jupiter's moons orbiting the giant planet. His observations showed us that Earth is not the center of everything, shifting our cosmic perspective.

His discoveries weren't welcomed by everyone, though. Galileo's views challenged the idea that Earth was the center of the Universe - a belief held by many, including the Church. He faced fierce opposition, even house arrest. But truth, like the stars, cannot be hidden forever.

So, next time you look through a telescope, remember Galileo. His courage and curiosity showed us our place in the Universe, turning that small tube into a powerful tool for discovery. Talk about a revolutionary gadget!

Fact 39 - Walking on Water in Space

Picture this, you're onboard the International Space Station (ISS), floating in mid-air. Your water bottle isn't on the table, it's bobbing next to you. As you reach out to grab it, a water droplet escapes, drifting away, and you watch it form a perfect sphere. Welcome to the strange world of zero gravity!

In space, with gravity's pull minimized, traditional rules don't apply. Water doesn't pour, it floats. Astronauts don't walk, they float too. Every object becomes weightless, leading to unusual and often mind-boggling sights. Ever watched someone 'walk on water'? In space, it's possible!

Yet, this zero-gravity environment isn't just about floating fun and games. It poses unique challenges too. Imagine trying to sleep without sinking into a mattress, or eating when your food doesn't stay on the plate. Even the human body behaves differently, with fluids in our cells redistributing, leading to a puffy face and spindly legs.

So, while you marvel at astronauts doing backflips and playing with floating bubbles, remember that living in zero gravity is a science and an art. It's a peculiar ballet of adaptation, ingenuity, and constant discovery. One giant leap, indeed!

Fact 40 - Oumuamua, The Alien Asteroid?

In 2017, a peculiar object zipped through our Solar System. Scientists named it 'Oumuamua', Hawaiian for 'scout'. Unlike asteroids or comets we've observed, Oumuamua didn't originate from our Solar System. It's an interstellar vagabond, a relic from another star system altogether. A space wanderer, if you will.

Oumuamua didn't just stand out due to its origins. Its shape and behavior were anomalies too. Stretching about 800 meters long but only 80 meters wide, its cigar-like form is unlike anything we've seen. Plus, its speed and trajectory couldn't be solely explained by the gravitational pull of the Sun and planets alone.

Speculations soared. Could it be an alien spacecraft, some asked. Most scientists, however, favor a natural explanation. The leading theory? It might be a fragment ejected from a distant star system during a planet's formation or due to a stellar explosion.

Whatever Oumuamua is, it's long gone now, moving away from the Sun at over 38 kilometers per second. It reminds us of the vast, unexplored mysteries of space, proving that sometimes, the cosmos does indeed send more than just whispers on the solar wind.

Fact 41 - Star within a Star

In the mind-bending theatre of cosmic wonders, Thorne-Zytkow objects (TZOs) might top the bill. They're essentially a star within a star — a concept that almost sounds like science fiction. Here's the gist: imagine a tiny but incredibly dense neutron star, swallowed by a much larger, giant or supergiant star.

These peculiar entities are named after Kip Thorne and Anna Zytkow, the astrophysicists who first proposed their existence in the 1970s. They speculated that these cosmic matryoshka dolls might form when a neutron star in a binary system is engulfed by its companion as the companion evolves and expands.

Thorne-Zytkow objects are believed to have unique chemical signatures. Due to their bizarre structure, the fusion processes in their interiors would produce heavy elements in different abundances than normal stars. This gives them their own spectral fingerprint, which can be detected from Earth.

As of my knowledge cutoff in 2021, no confirmed TZOs have been discovered. But astronomers have some promising candidates. If these objects do exist, they further highlight the astonishingly diverse cast of cosmic characters that populate our Universe.

Fact 42 - Billion Year Journeys: The Life of a Star

The life of a star is a saga spanning billions of years, beginning as a humble cloud of gas and dust. You might find it hard to believe, but that's exactly how our own Sun started its journey. The process that triggers the birth of a star is called gravitational collapse - when dense regions within a nebula, or cosmic cloud, succumb to their own gravity and begin to contract.

After millions of years of this relentless contraction, the core of the collapsing cloud heats up, initiating nuclear fusion and creating a protostar. The star then enters the longest stage of its life, the main sequence phase, where it steadily fuses hydrogen into helium, just like our Sun is doing right now.

Eventually, the star exhausts its hydrogen fuel. What happens next depends on the star's mass. It may swell into a red giant, cast off its outer layers and leave behind a white dwarf. Alternatively, if it's massive enough, it might explode in a supernova, potentially leaving behind a neutron star or a black hole.

Witnessing the life of a star is witnessing the universe's way of recycling matter, from one generation of stars to the next. As Carl Sagan famously said, "We're made of star stuff," and he meant it literally!

Fact 43 - Space Oddity: The Sounds of Space

Space, as you may know, is a vacuum, meaning it doesn't have a medium like air or water through which sound waves can travel. So, if you were to shout in the void of space, no one would hear you scream. But that doesn't mean space is silent. In fact, space is buzzing with "sounds" if we know where to listen.

These 'sounds' are electromagnetic waves that can be converted into sound waves. When spacecraft like NASA's Voyager and Juno captured radio emissions from celestial bodies, scientists converted them into audio files. The result is a set of eerie, alien-like whistles, whooshes, and roars.

For instance, the audio files of Jupiter are filled with swirling harmonic tones, while Saturn's radio emissions sound more like a rhythmic beat of a drum. And when you listen to the Earth's 'chorus', it resembles the chirping of tropical birds at dawn.

So, while space might be quiet in the traditional sense, the universe is humming its own cosmic symphony. It's just that our human ears aren't equipped to hear it directly. But with the right tools, we can tune in to the soundtrack of the cosmos.

Fact 44 - Goldilocks Planets

In the classic fairytale, Goldilocks was searching for the porridge, the chair, and the bed that were 'just right'. Similarly, in space, scientists are on the hunt for planets that are 'just right' for life as we know it. These planets, appropriately dubbed 'Goldilocks Planets', exist in what's called the 'habitable zone'.

The habitable zone, or the 'Goldilocks Zone', is the region around a star where conditions could be just right for liquid water to exist on a planet's surface. Too close to the star, and any water would evaporate; too far, it would freeze. But within this zone, life as we know it could potentially thrive.

Our own Earth is, of course, the most familiar Goldilocks planet. But with the advent of sophisticated space telescopes, scientists have started identifying other such planets in distant solar systems. Kepler-186f, for instance, is an exoplanet about 500 light years away that might just fit the bill.

So the quest continues for these 'just right' planets. And who knows? Perhaps, somewhere out there in the cosmic vastness, another Goldilocks planet is waiting to be discovered, complete with its own tale to tell.

Fact 45 - Stellar Corpses: The Dark World of Black Dwarfs

A star's life is a thing of wonder, from its fiery birth in a nebula to its ultimate fate. One possible end point, reserved for low to medium mass stars like our sun, is as a black dwarf. But don't be fooled by the name - these stellar remnants have a unique story to tell.

Black dwarfs are what white dwarfs become after they've exhausted their nuclear fuel and cooled down. White dwarfs are the glowing hot cores of dead stars, left behind after the outer layers have been shed. Over billions of years, these white dwarfs emit their stored heat and eventually cool down, turning into black dwarfs.

However, the universe is not old enough for any black dwarfs to exist yet. Even the oldest white dwarf still radiates heat, its surface temperature far hotter than any pot on your stove. Theoretical predictions suggest it may take longer than the current age of the universe for a white dwarf to cool into a black dwarf.

So while we cannot observe black dwarfs today, understanding their predicted existence allows us a fascinating glimpse into the distant future of the universe - a future where these silent, dark stellar corpses might eventually fill the sky.

Fact 46 - Why is Space Dark? The Olbers' Paradox

Gazing up at the night sky, you're met with a vast black canvas sprinkled with stars. But have you ever wondered, why is space dark? If the universe is infinite and filled with stars, shouldn't the sky be flooded with light? This conundrum is known as Olbers' Paradox.

The paradox takes its name from Heinrich Wilhelm Olbers, who discussed it in the 19th century, although it was considered by others before him. The question is based on the assumption that the universe is infinite, static, and filled uniformly with stars, causing every line of sight to eventually land on a star.

Yet the darkness of the night sky reveals this assumption isn't accurate. One resolution to the paradox is the idea that the universe is not infinitely old. Light from distant stars hasn't had time to reach us due to the finite speed of light. In essence, we're looking at a cosmic horizon.

Additionally, the ongoing expansion of the universe means distant stars and galaxies are redshifted, their light stretched to longer, dimmer wavelengths. So, while it may seem paradoxical, the darkness of space offers profound insights into the nature of the universe itself.

Fact 47 - The Moon's Dark Side: It's Not What You Think!

When you look up at the Moon, have you ever pondered what lies on the side you can't see? It's often referred to as the "dark side" of the Moon, but contrary to popular belief, it's not perpetually in darkness. Let's delve into this lunar enigma.

The term "dark side" is a misnomer and is more accurately described as the "far side". The Moon is tidally locked with Earth, meaning it rotates on its axis at the same rate that it orbits our planet. Therefore, we always see the same face, while the far side remains hidden from view.

Despite its nickname, the far side isn't devoid of sunlight. Like the side we see, it experiences a day-night cycle, receiving sunlight half the time. The "darkness" refers more to our lack of knowledge about this hidden half for a long time.

Our understanding of the far side improved dramatically in 1959 when the Soviet Luna 3 spacecraft transmitted the first images. Since then, numerous missions have expanded our knowledge, revealing a terrain heavily cratered and with fewer large lunar seas (maria) compared to the near side. This unseen side is not darker, just different!

Fact 48 - Shooting for the Stars: The Speed of a Rocket

When we speak about rockets, we often talk about their awe-inspiring power and their blazing speed. Have you ever wondered just how fast these mammoth machines must go to break free of Earth's gravitational clutches? Let's put things into perspective.

Achieving orbit isn't merely about going up; it's about going sideways fast enough. To stay in orbit, a spacecraft has to travel at a speed of about 28,000 kilometers per hour! This speed enables a balance between gravitational pull and the spacecraft's inertia, creating a continuous falling motion around Earth - essentially what an orbit is.

How about going beyond, to other planets or stars? That's where escape velocity comes in, the minimum speed an object needs to escape a planet's gravitational pull completely. For Earth, it's an astounding 40,270 kilometers per hour. But, remember, reaching such speeds isn't an easy task. It requires overcoming air resistance and carrying sufficient fuel.

So, next time you watch a rocket launch, know that you are witnessing an immense ballet of physics and engineering, where speed plays a crucial role in taking us beyond the boundaries of our planet and into the vastness of space.

Fact 49 - The Sky is Falling: The Danger of Space Junk

The beauty of a clear night sky may leave you in awe, but there's more to it than meets the eye. Beyond our atmosphere, in the infinity of space, orbits a growing cloud of man-made debris. Space junk, as it's commonly called, is a cause for concern and a potential threat to both space and ground-based infrastructure.

Space junk includes defunct satellites, spent rocket stages, and fragments from disintegration and collision events. As of now, there are about 128 million pieces of debris smaller than 1 cm, around 900,000 pieces of debris 1–10 cm, and around 34,000 of pieces larger than 10 cm. These objects whiz around the Earth at speeds up to 28,000 kilometers per hour.

At such high velocities, even a small piece of debris can cause catastrophic damage to a functioning satellite or space station. On the ground, space junk can pose a threat if it re-enters the Earth's atmosphere and crashes. While most debris will burn up during re-entry, some larger objects might survive and reach the surface.

Efforts to mitigate the space junk problem are ongoing. Techniques like deorbiting defunct satellites and capturing debris are being explored. Remember, as we reach for the stars, we must also be careful not to clutter the path.

Fact 50 - Twinkle Twinkle, Variable Star

Not all stars maintain a constant shine. Some stars, known as variable stars, exhibit a fascinating trait — their brightness changes over time. If you've ever wondered if the stars are subtly playing tricks on your eyes, you're not mistaken.

Variable stars' brightness changes are due to internal or external factors. Pulsating variable stars, for example, change their brightness due to periodic swelling and shrinking of the star's outer layers. On the other hand, eclipsing binary stars vary in brightness because of the motion of one star in front of the other, blocking some or all of its light.

In the grand cosmic theater, variable stars play a vital role. For astronomers, these stars are valuable tools for measuring cosmic distances. The predictable patterns of certain variable stars, like Cepheids and RR Lyrae stars, provide a 'cosmic yardstick' for gauging the size of the universe.

So, the next time you gaze at the night sky, appreciate the dynamic dance of the variable stars. They are not just twinkling, but telling tales of cosmic proportions. From minute pulsations to grand celestial eclipses, their rhythmic variations illuminate our understanding of the universe.

Fact 51 - The Heaviest Stars: Meet the Hypergiants

Among the multitude of stars in the universe, some truly stand out. Enter the hypergiants - the universe's heavyweight champions. Far larger and brighter than ordinary stars, these celestial giants sit at the top of the stellar weight class.

Hypergiants are rare stars that have masses around 10 to 50 times that of our Sun. But what really sets them apart is their luminosity. They are incredibly bright, shining up to a million times brighter than the Sun. These gigantic stars dominate their surroundings, casting a powerful cosmic glow.

However, such grandeur comes with a price. Hypergiants live fast and die young. Their intense brightness is a sign of their furious energy consumption. They burn through their nuclear fuel at a mind-boggling pace, leading to a lifespan that is significantly shorter than less massive stars.

In their death throes, hypergiants often explode in spectacular supernovae, sometimes even creating black holes. They are a testament to the grand scale of the universe and the awe-inspiring forces at work in the cosmos. So, as you gaze up at the night sky, remember the hypergiants - the universe's shining titans.

Fact 52 - Saturn's Ravioli: The Oddly Shaped Moon Pan

The universe is brimming with objects that constantly defy expectations, and Saturn's moon Pan is a prime example. Tucked away within Saturn's stunning rings, Pan has earned a rather appetizing moniker - it's often compared to a ravioli due to its unique shape.

Only about 35 kilometers across, Pan orbits within Saturn's A ring in a region known as the Encke Gap. Unlike the spherical shape commonly associated with moons, Pan is best described as having a shape similar to a walnut or ravioli, with a bulging equator and slim polar regions.

This unusual structure is a result of Pan's location within Saturn's rings. The moon's equatorial ridge is made up of particles from the ring system that have accreted onto its surface over millions of years, creating the distinct 'ravioli' shape that we see today.

So the next time you're enjoying a plate of ravioli, remember that a similar shape is floating in the void of space, tracing its lonely path around Saturn. Pan is a testament to the diverse and often unexpected forms that celestial bodies can take.

Fact 53 - Space Elevator: The Future of Space Travel?

The notion of a space elevator might sound like it's straight out of a sci-fi novel, but some scientists believe it could revolutionize space travel. This ambitious concept involves building a colossal tether from Earth's surface extending directly into space.

The space elevator would work by using a counterweight stationed beyond geostationary orbit, holding the cable taut by centrifugal force. Climbers, akin to elevator cars, would ascend the tether, eliminating the need for costly and environmentally harmful rocket launches.

Challenges are plenty, from manufacturing a material strong and light enough for the tether, to avoiding space debris and weather phenomena. Currently, carbon nanotubes and diamond nanothreads are considered potential materials due to their exceptional strength and lightness, but producing them in the needed quantities remains a hurdle.

Nevertheless, if realized, a space elevator could drastically reduce the cost and risk associated with reaching space. It's a testament to human ingenuity and our relentless pursuit to make the cosmos more accessible, transforming space travel from a daring adventure into a routine commute.

Fact 54 - Our Nearest Star Neighbor: The Proxima Centauri

Have you ever wondered what lies beyond our solar system? Meet Proxima Centauri, our nearest star neighbor. Located a mere 4.24 light-years away, this red dwarf star is a part of the Alpha Centauri system, despite being 0.21 light-years away from Alpha Centauri A and B.

Proxima Centauri is an M-type star, smaller and cooler than our Sun. It has an apparent magnitude of 11, which means it's too faint to be seen with the naked eye. Despite its proximity, it was only discovered in 1915 by Robert Innes due to its low luminosity.

Interestingly, Proxima Centauri is home to at least two exoplanets. One of these, Proxima Centauri b, lies within the star's habitable zone, meaning liquid water could potentially exist on its surface, a key ingredient for life as we know it.

Although Proxima Centauri's proximity makes it a tempting target for future interstellar travel, the journey would still take thousands of years with current technology. It serves as a humbling reminder of the vastness of our cosmos and the long journey we've yet to embark on.

Fact 55 - Bizarre Alignment: The Oddity of Uranus' Tilt

Let's take a tour of our peculiar planetary neighbor, Uranus. Unlike the other planets in our solar system, Uranus spins on its side, exhibiting a bizarre tilt of about 98 degrees. This peculiar axial tilt causes some unusual weather and lighting patterns on the planet.

In most planets, their axis of rotation is more or less perpendicular to the plane of their orbit. However, Uranus looks as if it's rolling around the Sun on its side. Scientists believe this unusual tilt may have resulted from a colossal collision with an Earth-sized object in the distant past.

This sideways orientation leads to extreme seasons. Each pole gets around 42 years of continuous sunlight, followed by 42 years of darkness. Imagine a day that lasts half your lifetime, followed by a night of the same length.

Uranus' tilt makes it a unique object of study for astronomers. It serves as a reminder that the universe is full of oddities and exceptions to the rule, stimulating our curiosity and desire to uncover the mysteries of the cosmos.

Fact 56 - A Tale of Two Suns: Binary Star Systems

Ever imagined what it would be like to live on a planet with two suns? This might not be just a fantasy. In the universe, many stars exist in binary systems – a celestial dance where two stars orbit around their common center of mass.

In these systems, the two stars may be of similar size, or one could be significantly larger than the other. Depending on the system, the stars could be so close that they share a common envelope of gas, or they could be so far apart that it takes centuries for them to orbit around each other.

For inhabitants of a hypothetical planet in a binary system, the night sky would be a mesmerizing spectacle. Depending on the orbital characteristics, they might witness the two suns rising and setting together, or they might see one during the day and the other during the night, offering a persistent daylight.

The concept of binary systems not only broadens our perspective of the cosmic diversity but also influences the search for habitable exoplanets. They're another testament to the fascinating and varied architecture of the universe.

Fact 57 - Bubble Nebula: The Beauty of Stellar Nurseries

At a glance, the cosmos may seem silent and static. However, it's constantly changing, creating and destroying on grand scales. One of the most spectacular examples of cosmic creation is the Bubble Nebula, also known as NGC 7635, a literal nursery for new stars.

Located about 7,100 light-years away in the constellation Cassiopeia, the Bubble Nebula is an emission nebula — a gigantic cloud of ionized gas that emits its own light. Its stunning shape, akin to a soap bubble, is created by stellar wind from a massive hot, young central star.

Inside this radiant bubble, stars are born from dense clumps of gas and dust. As these areas collapse under their own gravity, the pressure and temperature in their core rises, eventually sparking nuclear fusion and giving birth to a new star. The sight of these starry cradles is a wonder to behold.

By studying nebulae like the Bubble Nebula, astronomers hope to learn more about how stars are formed, helping us understand the life cycles of stars, and in turn, the evolution of galaxies and the universe itself. These celestial nurseries truly are a beautiful spectacle of cosmic creation.

Fact 58 - Einstein's Proven Right

Albert Einstein, one of the most brilliant minds in human history, proposed an intriguing prediction in his General Theory of Relativity over a century ago: the existence of gravitational waves. It wasn't until 2015, a hundred years later, that this theory was confirmed, adding a new chapter to our understanding of the universe.

Gravitational waves are ripples in the fabric of space-time caused by the movements of massive objects, such as black holes or neutron stars. Picture a stone thrown into a pond, creating waves that travel across the water's surface, except in this case, the pond is the universe itself.

The detection of these waves was a technological triumph. Scientists at the LIGO (Laser Interferometer Gravitational-Wave Observatory) were able to measure tiny disturbances, less than the width of a proton, caused by these waves passing through Earth. This groundbreaking discovery opened up a whole new way to observe the cosmos.

Gravitational waves provide a unique lens through which we can study the universe, giving us a way to witness cosmic events that were previously hidden. Once again, Einstein's genius was proven right, and our understanding of the universe took a giant leap forward.

Fact 59 - The Intriguing Stellar Ballet

Ever looked up at the night sky and marveled at the constellations, those beautiful patterns of stars that seem so still and unchanging? In truth, there's a celestial dance happening right above you. Stars, just like you and everything else in the universe, are in constant motion. It's a stellar ballet, choreographed by the force of gravity.

Stars orbit the center of their galaxies, following a path determined by the collective gravitational pull of all the matter within the galaxy. Our sun, for example, is cruising along at a speed of about 220 kilometers per second as it orbits the center of the Milky Way.

But it's not just a simple orbit. Stars can also dance in pairs or groups, bound together by their mutual gravity. These are called binary or multiple star systems. Some of them engage in a mesmerizing cosmic waltz, exchanging material and dramatically affecting each other's evolution.

So, the next time you gaze at the starry sky, remember: you're not just looking at distant points of light, but a dynamic, ever-moving cosmic ballet. It's a performance billions of years in the making, and you've got a front-row seat.

Fact 60 - Cosmic Beast: The Voracious Quasars

In the vast cosmic wilderness, there exists a type of celestial object so bright and powerful, it outshines entire galaxies. Meet the quasars, or quasi-stellar objects, some of the most energetic entities in the known universe. Yet, they're no larger than our solar system, a testament to their astonishing potency.

Quasars lie at the hearts of certain galaxies, where a supermassive black hole is continuously feeding on surrounding matter. As the black hole devours gas, dust, and stars, the material spirals inward, forming an extremely hot accretion disk. The intense gravitational and frictional forces within this disk generate an incredible amount of light and energy.

In their prime, quasars can emit thousands of times the total light output of our Milky Way, making them visible across billions of light-years. Astronomers use them as cosmic beacons to study the early universe, as the light we observe from quasars today began its journey when the universe was still young.

So, when you think of the cosmos' most powerful phenomena, consider the voracious quasars. Hidden within galaxies, these cosmic beasts feast relentlessly, illuminating the distant corners of our universe with their insatiable hunger.

Fact 61 - The Enigmatic Cosmic Strings

In the complex tapestry of the cosmos, certain threads weave an even deeper mystery. These are cosmic strings - theoretical topological defects in the fabric of spacetime, akin to cracks formed on a frozen pond. While we're still hunting for evidence of their existence, they could offer profound insights into the fundamental nature of our universe.

These hypothetical strings, less than a proton's width but potentially spanning light-years in length, are remnants of the early universe. They're believed to have formed during the phase transitions following the Big Bang, when the cosmos cooled and the fundamental forces separated. Cosmic strings carry substantial mass, exerting a powerful gravitational effect on their surroundings.

These strings, if they exist, would warp spacetime in unique ways, creating distinct signatures in the cosmic microwave background or generating gravitational waves. Finding these imprints would provide critical tests of string theory, a proposed "theory of everything" that unites quantum mechanics and general relativity.

So, next time you gaze up at the stars, consider the hidden threads that might lurk in the cosmic shadows - the enigmatic cosmic strings. In their elusive simplicity, they hold keys to understanding the grandest mysteries of the universe.

Fact 62 - Cosmic Artwork: The Splendid Northern Lights

Take a moment and imagine yourself under the clear dark sky, far from the city's hustle, when suddenly the sky lights up with ethereal waves of color, creating an impressionist masterpiece. This is not a figment of your imagination, but the Northern Lights, or Aurora Borealis, one of the most breathtaking natural spectacles.

Born from a cosmic dance between the Earth's magnetic field and solar particles, these shimmering curtains of light are most commonly seen near the Earth's polar regions. As charged particles from the Sun collide with atmospheric gases, they create glowing ripples of green, red, yellow, blue, and purple across the night sky.

Each color of the Northern Lights is a signature of a particular gas being excited by solar particles. The most common green color is produced by oxygen molecules located about 60 miles above Earth, while nitrogen produces blue or purplish-red auroras.

So, when you look up at the Northern Lights, remember you're witnessing a celestial ballet of particles and magnetic fields, painting the canvas of our sky. It's a testament to the universe's ability to create astonishing beauty from even its most violent events.

Fact 63 - The Tallest Mountain in Space

You may have heard of Mount Everest, the tallest mountain on Earth, but have you ever wondered about the tallest mountain in the entire solar system? Look no further than Mars, home to the colossal Olympus Mons, a shield volcano that dwarfs every mountain on Earth.

Standing an astonishing 13.6 miles high, Olympus Mons is nearly three times the height of Mount Everest. The base of this gigantic mountain is roughly equivalent to the size of the state of Arizona in the U.S., making it not only the tallest, but also one of the broadest volcanoes known.

The sheer size of Olympus Mons is due to the static nature of the Martian crust. On Earth, the movement of tectonic plates prevents the buildup of magma in one place. But on Mars, the lava flows for millions of years at a single hotspot, piling up to form this enormous mountain.

Next time you gaze at the Red Planet, remember, you're also looking at the home of the tallest mountain known to humanity. The Olympus Mons is one of the many marvels that make Mars a fascinating destination for future exploration.

Fact 64 - The Ultimate Time Machine: The Hubble Telescope

When you gaze at the stars, did you know you're also looking back in time? Light from distant stars takes years to reach our eyes, so we see them as they were in the past. This concept is taken to the extreme by the Hubble Space Telescope, a veritable time machine that lets us peer billions of years into the universe's history.

Launched in 1990, Hubble orbits Earth, far above the distortion of our atmosphere, capturing clear images of deep space. Its spectacular observations range from nearby planets to galaxies billions of light-years away. The farther Hubble looks, the further back in time it sees.

Hubble's contributions to science are innumerable. It helped determine the rate of the universe's expansion, observed the atmospheres of distant exoplanets, and captured the earliest galaxies forming just 400 million years after the Big Bang. Its images have not only expanded our scientific knowledge but also captivated us with their breathtaking beauty.

So next time you look at a Hubble image, remember you're not just seeing a distant part of space, but also a glimpse into the universe's past. The Hubble Telescope truly is our ultimate time machine.

Fact 65 - An Ocean in Space: Jupiter's Moon Europa

Can you imagine an ocean in space? Well, you don't have to! Meet Europa, one of Jupiter's largest moons, which scientists believe hides a vast ocean beneath its icy surface. This makes Europa one of the most intriguing bodies in our solar system, a possible home for extraterrestrial life.

Europa's surface is a frozen shell covered in a mosaic of cracks and ridges, indicating movement from beneath. Scientists suspect a salty ocean, possibly twice the volume of all Earth's oceans combined, exists beneath this icy exterior. The heat required to maintain this liquid state is likely provided by the gravitational interaction with Jupiter and its other moons.

These conditions lead to speculation that Europa's ocean may harbor life. The ocean, warmed by the moon's internal heat and enriched with chemicals from the ice and possible volcanic activity on the seafloor, could provide the necessary environment for life to exist.

Europa, an ocean moon, is a testament to the wonders of our solar system. The possibility of life existing in its depths is tantalizing, turning Europa into a key target for future space missions. Can you imagine what secrets Europa might reveal?

Fact 66 - The Spiral Marvel: The Andromeda Galaxy

Have you ever gazed into the night sky and seen a faint, misty patch, barely visible to the naked eye? If so, you've witnessed the Andromeda Galaxy, the closest spiral galaxy to the Milky Way and one of the few galaxies visible without a telescope.

At an estimated 2.5 million light-years away, Andromeda is our galactic neighbor. It is the largest galaxy in our Local Group, which also includes the Milky Way, the Triangulum Galaxy, and about 54 other smaller galaxies. It is an awe-inspiring spectacle with its spiral arms and glowing center, containing approximately one trillion stars.

What makes Andromeda so fascinating is its inevitable destiny. Astronomers predict that in about 4.5 billion years, Andromeda and the Milky Way will collide to form a single, elliptical galaxy. This dramatic cosmic event, fortunately, is so far in the future that life on Earth is unlikely to be affected.

Andromeda is a testament to the grand scale and beauty of the universe. Its sheer size, spiraling structure, and destined collision with the Milky Way are captivating reminders of the dynamic and ever-evolving cosmos we are part of.

Fact 67 - Through the Wormhole

Have you ever imagined traveling across vast cosmic distances in an instant? Wormholes, theoretically, could make this seemingly impossible feat possible. They are fascinating structures that might exist in the fabric of spacetime, creating shortcuts between two distant points in the universe.

These hypothetical 'tunnels' in spacetime have been popularized by science fiction and were initially posited by physicist Albert Einstein and Nathan Rosen in 1935 as part of their theory of general relativity. Wormholes have yet to be observed, but they remain a vibrant area of research, particularly in theories like quantum gravity.

For wormholes to be traversable, they'd have to be 'stabilized' by something known as 'exotic matter', a type of material with negative energy density, also still theoretical. Without it, a wormhole would collapse in the blink of an eye, destroying anything attempting to pass through it.

Although wormholes are still purely theoretical, their existence would have profound implications for our understanding of the universe. Could they be the key to interstellar travel, or even time travel? We don't know yet, but studying them pushes the boundaries of our understanding of the universe.

Fact 68 - Sailing on Light: The Dream of Solar Sailing

Imagine harnessing the power of the sun to sail across the universe, unbound by the constraints of fuel. Solar sailing, an intriguing concept in space exploration, is precisely this idea, using the pressure exerted by sunlight as a means of propulsion.

Solar sails function much like the sails of a ship, but instead of wind, they capture the momentum of photons, particles of light emitted by the sun. When these photons strike the sail, they transfer their momentum, providing a continuous, if slight, thrust. Over time, this tiny push can accelerate a spacecraft to high speeds.

This idea isn't confined to the realm of theory. The Japan Aerospace Exploration Agency (JAXA) successfully deployed a solar sail on its IKAROS mission in 2010. More recently, the non-profit organization The Planetary Society launched LightSail 2, another solar sail spacecraft, in 2019.

Solar sailing offers an incredibly fuel-efficient way to explore our universe, though challenges like managing the sail's orientation and creating a sufficiently lightweight yet durable material remain. Still, as we learn to harness the sun's power, we move one step closer to voyages of unlimited duration and distance.

Fact 69 - Blue Planet's Red Twin: The Planet Mars

Look up at the night sky and you may spot a reddish, non-twinkling dot. That's Mars, Earth's 'red twin.' Though it's often associated with legends and myths, Mars is a fascinating world of scientific discovery.

Mars, named after the Roman god of war due to its blood-red hue, is often called Earth's twin because of their similarities. It has polar ice caps made of water and carbon dioxide, much like Earth's polar ice caps, and a day on Mars (a 'sol') is only a little over 24 hours, nearly similar to Earth's 24-hour day.

The surface of Mars is a vast, barren desert marked by towering volcanoes, deep canyons, and impact craters. Olympus Mons, the tallest volcano in the solar system, calls Mars home. The planet also shows evidence of ancient river valleys and lakes, suggesting a wetter past and prompting scientists to question whether life could have once existed there.

Despite its harsh, cold conditions now, Mars continues to captivate us. With ongoing exploration from rovers like Perseverance and the potential for human missions in the future, Mars remains a beacon of exploration and the potential for discovery in our solar system.

Fact 70 - Interstellar Winds: The Breezes in Space

When you imagine the vast emptiness of space, the concept of wind may seem rather misplaced. But did you know that space isn't as empty as we perceive it to be? It is filled with what scientists refer to as interstellar winds, a crucial player in the cosmic stage.

Interstellar wind is a stream of charged particles, mostly protons and electrons, ejected by stars in all directions. This 'wind' flows through space, constantly shaping and reshaping the interstellar medium, the space between stars filled with sparse particles and radiation.

Our Sun contributes its own share to these cosmic breezes through solar wind. Emanating from the Sun's corona, it expands in all directions, reaching far beyond the orbits of the outermost planets. This wind creates a bubble around our solar system, known as the heliosphere, protecting us from harmful cosmic rays from deep space.

The discovery and ongoing study of interstellar winds provide valuable insight into our universe's dynamics. They shape galaxies, trigger star formation, and even affect planetary atmospheres. These breezes in space are truly more influential than they might first appear.

Fact 71 - Cosmic Wonders: The Incredible Pillars of Creation

As you marvel at the wonders of the universe, one sight stands out for its majestic beauty and scale - the Pillars of Creation. These fascinating structures, located in the Eagle Nebula, are cosmic nurseries where new stars are born, illuminating the darkness of space with their brilliance.

Named for their tall, pillar-like structures, the Pillars of Creation stretch across about 5 light-years. These towers of cosmic dust and gas are regions of intense star formation. They're dense enough to collapse under their own gravity, leading to the formation of young, bright stars within.

The Pillars were first captured in 1995 by the Hubble Space Telescope, and their stunning image has since become one of the most iconic pictures of space. The pillars' eerie, luminescent quality is due to the ultraviolet light from young, hot stars causing the gas within the pillars to glow.

Despite their serenity, these Pillars are sites of dramatic, dynamic change, an embodiment of the universe's continuous creation and destruction cycle. They represent the wonder and vastness of our universe, standing as magnificent markers of space's star-forming processes.

Fact 72 - Space Serpent: The Twisting Draco Constellation

As you gaze at the night sky, you can spot the Draco constellation twisting through the Northern Hemisphere. Known as the Dragon, Draco is a sprawling constellation that coils around the North Star, lending it the appearance of a cosmic serpent dancing amidst the stars.

The Draco constellation is rich in myth and legend. Its name comes from the Latin term for dragon, and it has been a staple in celestial folklore for centuries. The ancient Greeks saw it as Ladon, the dragon guarding Hera's golden apples in the garden of Hesperides, while Chinese astronomers visualized it as a tortoise or snake.

Draco is home to a wide range of celestial objects, including the Cat's Eye Nebula, an intriguingly complex planetary nebula. Another fascinating object is the Draco Dwarf Galaxy, one of the faintest galaxies known, and a satellite of our Milky Way.

Through a small telescope, you can explore Draco's wealth of galaxies, nebulae, and binary stars. The dragon constellation is a celestial marvel that connects us with ancient cultures, offering a glimpse into the universe's distant corners and our shared human history.

Fact 73 - The Richest Asteroid in the Universe

Imagine a rock so loaded with precious metals and diamonds that its worth surpasses the entire global economy. Welcome to the incredible world of 16 Psyche, an asteroid residing in the main asteroid belt between Mars and Jupiter. This gem-studded celestial body, with a diameter of around 140 miles, is thought to be the richest asteroid in our Solar System.

Made primarily of iron and nickel, Psyche is unique. Unlike most asteroids, which are rocky or icy, Psyche is thought to be the leftover core of a planet that never fully formed. Spectral analysis suggests it may also contain precious metals such as gold and platinum, and perhaps even diamonds, produced by the asteroid's tumultuous history.

The immense value of 16 Psyche has naturally stirred curiosity and ambition. NASA has plans to launch a mission to Psyche, aiming to arrive by 2026. This mission will provide a unique opportunity to explore a planetary core up close.

16 Psyche is a celestial treasure trove that sparks our imagination. As you look up at the night sky, remember that there's a potential quadrillion-dollar asteroid spinning silently in the darkness, just waiting to be explored.

Fact 74 - The Spinning Top: The Rapid Rotation of Pulsars

In the vast expanse of the cosmos, many objects whirl at impressive speeds. None more so than pulsars, the rapidly rotating neutron stars that outpace even the most skilled ballerina or the quickest spin of a top. Pulsars, the collapsed remnants of massive stars after supernovae, are among the most extreme objects in the universe.

Their dizzying rotational speed is due to the conservation of angular momentum. When a massive star implodes, its core shrinks drastically in size but its angular momentum remains constant. Like a figure skater pulling in her arms to spin faster, the collapsed star's rotation speed increases dramatically, resulting in pulsars that can rotate hundreds of times per second!

Pulsars emit powerful beams of electromagnetic radiation from their magnetic poles. As they spin, these beams sweep across the universe like the beam of a lighthouse. When the beam points towards Earth, we detect a pulse of radiation, giving these stars their name - pulsars.

So the next time you watch a top spin or a dancer twirl, remember the pulsars, cosmic spinning tops that put everything else in the shade. Their remarkable rotation showcases the fascinating extremes of our universe.

Fact 75 - The Other Earths: The Habitable Exoplanets

Imagine finding another planet like ours, a mirror Earth in the vastness of space. The hunt for exoplanets—planets outside our solar system—is driven by this tantalizing possibility. Some of these distant worlds, termed "habitable exoplanets," are of particular interest. They reside in their star's habitable zone, the Goldilocks region not too hot or too cold, where liquid water could potentially exist.

The Kepler Space Telescope, a mission specifically designed to find exoplanets, has identified thousands, some of which reside in the habitable zone. One of the most famous is Kepler-22b, orbiting in the habitable zone of a star similar to our own sun. Though its true nature remains unknown, its potential for Earth-like conditions stirs our imaginations.

Technology continues to evolve, enhancing our capabilities in this cosmic treasure hunt. With the recent deployment of NASA's James Webb Space Telescope, our capacity to scrutinize these distant worlds in greater detail than ever before has grown immensely.

We're on the precipice of discovering whether we're truly alone in the universe. If we find a second Earth, a habitable exoplanet, it would be a revelation, altering our understanding of our place in the cosmos forever.

Fact 76 - Solar System's Guard: The Asteroid Belt

When you gaze up at the night sky, you're likely not thinking about the clutter of rocky debris orbiting between Mars and Jupiter. Welcome to the asteroid belt, our solar system's guard, a vast ring of rocky remnants from the early solar system.

Despite images of dense, dangerous fields of rocks, the asteroid belt is actually quite sparse. The average distance between asteroids is a whopping 600,000 miles! So, spacecrafts like the numerous ones sent by NASA have safely traversed it without incident.

The asteroid belt is more than a space hazard, it's a historical archive. These primordial rocks, largely undisturbed for billions of years, hold secrets about the early solar system. Missions such as NASA's DAWN have visited large asteroids like Vesta and dwarf planet Ceres, revealing incredible insights.

So, the next time you look up at the night sky, remember the asteroid belt, our silent guardian. It not only divides the inner and outer solar system but also serves as a gateway to understanding our cosmic past. It's not just a belt of rocks, but a belt of knowledge, waiting to be discovered.

Fact 77 - Sun's Evil Twin: The Nemesis Star Theory

Does our Sun have an evil twin named Nemesis? The Nemesis Star Theory might sound like a plot from a science fiction novel, but it's a scientific hypothesis that has intrigued astronomers for decades.

The theory of the Nemesis star emerged in the 1980s when scientists noticed a peculiar pattern - mass extinctions on Earth seemed to occur in a cyclical pattern every 26 million years. Some researchers proposed a wild idea: a yet-undiscovered dwarf star, dubbed "Nemesis," in a highly elliptical orbit around the sun causing comet showers and subsequent extinctions on Earth.

However, our extensive sky surveys like the Two Micron All Sky Survey (2MASS) and the Wide-field Infrared Survey Explorer (WISE) have so far found no evidence of such a star. This lack of evidence has led many in the scientific community to doubt the Nemesis hypothesis.

Still, the Nemesis Star Theory is a fascinating example of how astronomers use clues from our planet and the broader cosmos to develop hypotheses about the universe. Whether fact or fiction, Nemesis reminds us that the universe is full of mysteries yet to be solved.

Fact 78 - Lonely Wanderer: The Journey of Voyager 1

Launched in 1977, Voyager 1 is a symbol of human achievement and curiosity. This spacecraft, as lonely as it may be, is on a profound mission that spans beyond our comprehension: a journey into interstellar space, the great beyond of our solar system.

You might be wondering what's so special about Voyager 1. Well, it's the farthest man-made object from Earth, currently over 14 billion miles away. It carries a golden record, a time capsule filled with sounds, images, and languages from Earth, intended for any extraterrestrial life forms that might come across it.

In 2012, Voyager 1 made headlines by becoming the first spacecraft to officially enter interstellar space, crossing the heliopause, where the solar wind from our sun slows down and merges with the interstellar medium. This marked a historic moment in space exploration.

While it may be a lonely wanderer, Voyager 1 is not entirely alone. We're still in contact, receiving data about cosmic rays, magnetic fields, and the interstellar medium. It's a testament to our desire to explore, to understand the universe, and to leave a mark, however small, on the cosmic ocean.

Fact 79 - The Sun's Furious Storm: Solar Flares

Did you know that our calm-looking Sun often throws a fit? Solar flares, the Sun's temper tantrums, are violent explosions on the solar surface releasing energy equivalent to millions of hydrogen bombs. These flares eject streams of electrons, ions, and atoms into space, producing a spectacle of light and radiation.

Solar flares are born from the Sun's magnetic energy. When magnetic fields twist and cross each other, they can explode and cause these flares. This violent process is part of the Sun's 11-year solar cycle, during which solar activity increases and decreases.

The aftermath of a solar flare is truly breathtaking. You may have seen images of the auroras – the Northern and Southern Lights. These beautiful phenomena occur when charged particles from solar flares interact with Earth's magnetic field, creating a mesmerizing light show in the sky.

But it's not all beauty and light. Solar flares can disrupt radio communications, cause damage to satellites, and even affect electrical power grids on Earth. However, our atmosphere largely protects us from harmful radiation. So while our Sun might have its furious moments, we can admire them from the safety of our planet.

Fact 80 - The Hottest and Coldest: Temperatures in Space

Did you know that space is a world of extremes, particularly when it comes to temperature? It might be hard to imagine, but space can be both unimaginably hot and bone-chillingly cold, and sometimes these extremes exist surprisingly close together.

The temperature in space largely depends on whether an area is in sunlight or shadow. In direct sunlight, temperatures can soar up to 250 degrees Celsius (482 degrees Fahrenheit). This is hot enough to boil water! On the other hand, in the shadow, away from the Sun's rays, temperatures can plummet to a frosty -250 degrees Celsius (-418 degrees Fahrenheit).

Interestingly, the coldest place in the universe is not in the shadowy depths of space, but on Earth. Inside a laboratory, scientists have achieved temperatures a billion times colder than the void of space! Conversely, the hottest temperatures ever recorded exist inside stars, where nuclear fusion takes place.

This extreme range of temperatures shapes the environment and conditions for all objects and events in space, from the orbits of planets to the formation of stars. Understanding these temperature extremes can help us unlock more secrets of the universe.

Fact 81 - Mirror, Mirror in the Sky: The Milky Way's Twin

When you gaze up at the night sky, did you know that you're looking at a cosmic doppelgänger? Among the hundreds of billions of galaxies in the universe, NGC 6744 has been identified as the Milky Way's twin. Just as beautiful, just as mysterious, yet strikingly similar in structure and appearance.

NGC 6744, located about 30 million light-years away in the southern constellation Pavo, is nearly identical to our home galaxy. It's a barred spiral galaxy, like the Milky Way, stretching approximately 200,000 light-years across—nearly twice as wide as our own galaxy.

What makes this doppelgänger truly remarkable is its spiral arms. Just like the Milky Way, NGC 6744 has several long, sweeping arms that are dotted with young blue stars, clouds of gas, and pockets of cosmic dust. It also has a central bar-shaped structure made of stars, giving it an appearance eerily similar to artistic representations of our galaxy.

The discovery of NGC 6744 has provided astronomers with a unique opportunity to see our own galaxy as if from the outside, aiding in our understanding of the Milky Way's structure and formation. So, while we can't step outside our galaxy to take a look, we can gaze upon our cosmic twin and see a mirror of our own celestial home.

Fact 82 - The Celestial Dance: The Magic of Solar Eclipses

Do you appreciate a good dance? What about one that takes place in the sky? The dance of celestial bodies during a solar eclipse is one of the most captivating phenomena in the universe. It's a ballet of the sun, moon, and earth, choreographed by gravity and orbits, captivating observers on Earth with its rarity and beauty.

Solar eclipses occur when the moon passes between the Earth and the sun, temporarily blocking the sun's light. This celestial alignment is a perfect dance, orchestrated by the clockwork precision of our solar system. The result? A breathtaking spectacle as day briefly turns into night, and a dazzling solar corona becomes visible.

The sight of a solar eclipse has been treasured since ancient times. Cultures around the world have spun myths and legends around this celestial event, from dragons eating the sun to divine omens. Today, eclipses are a prized event for astronomers and sky watchers, offering a unique opportunity to study the sun's outer atmosphere.

While they only occur a few times a year in varying locations, the magic of solar eclipses never fades. They serve as a stunning reminder of our place in the cosmos and the celestial dance that continues overhead, whether we're watching or not.

Fact 83 - The Extravagant Weather on Neptune

Have you ever wished for diamond rain? On Neptune, the eighth planet in our solar system, this wish is a weather forecast. Yes, you read it right! The deep blue gas giant is home to a most unusual form of precipitation — falling diamonds.

Neptune's atmosphere is largely composed of hydrogen and helium, with traces of methane that give it its deep blue color. But deeper within the planet, immense pressure and heat compress methane — which consists of carbon and hydrogen — into pure diamond crystals. These dazzling gems then precipitate like rain, sinking further into Neptune's core.

These diamond rains are thought to be responsible for an unusual excess heat emanating from Neptune. As diamonds descend and settle towards the planet's core, they release gravitational energy as heat. This constant drizzle of gems, perpetually warmed by the planet's interior, is a key to Neptune's atmospheric dynamics.

The diamond rain on Neptune is an extravagant demonstration of the universe's capacity for wonder, surpassing even the most fantastic imaginations. So the next time you gaze at the night sky, remember: in the depths of Neptune, it's raining diamonds.

Fact 84 - Cosmic Loners: The Rogue Planets

Ever heard of a planet without a star? In the vast, dark depths of interstellar space, lurk these celestial orphans, aptly named "rogue planets." Unlike the planets you're familiar with, rogues aren't gravitationally tied to any star or stellar remnant, free to wander the cosmic abyss.

Rogue planets are intriguing. Scientists think they are born in one of two ways: either they form in the chaotic environments of young star systems and get ejected, or they form directly from the collapse of dense interstellar gas clouds, just like stars do, but without enough mass to ignite fusion.

Despite their solitary nature, rogue planets are not doomed to eternal darkness. Some of these loners may have moons that produce heat through tidal forces, potentially warming up the surface of the planet and maintaining subsurface oceans, similar to Jupiter's moon Europa. If such conditions exist, life might find a way.

The concept of rogue planets reminds us of the limitless possibilities of the universe. These lone voyagers of the cosmos continue to defy our understanding and push the boundaries of what we consider a "planet" to be.

Fact 85 - The Birth of the Moon: Earth's Big Whack

Let's journey back in time to the tumultuous early years of the solar system, over 4 billion years ago. This is when a cosmic event of unimaginable proportions occurred, shaping the night sky as you know it today. The event is referred to as "The Big Whack" or "The Giant Impact," and it gave birth to our Moon.

The protagonist of this event was Theia, a Mars-sized body that roamed the early solar system. In a moment of cosmic fate, Theia slammed into the young Earth. The cataclysmic impact vaporized Theia and a part of Earth, with the debris flung into orbit around our planet.

In the aftermath of this colossal impact, the debris began to coalesce and slowly form the early Moon. This 'newborn' Moon was much closer to Earth and has been drifting away ever since. The scars of this violent origin are still visible as the Moon's craters.

The Big Whack theory explains many of the Moon's unique features and characteristics, including its size relative to Earth, its composition, and its lack of an iron-rich core. It serves as a stark reminder of the violent and chaotic beginnings of our serene-looking celestial companion.

Fact 86 - The Fascinating Exoplanet Kepler-22b

Imagine a world twice the size of Earth, shrouded in thick clouds and possibly covered by a global ocean. Welcome to Kepler-22b, a distant exoplanet that has piqued the curiosity of scientists and astronomers. Known as a "super-Earth," Kepler-22b orbits its host star, Kepler-22, located approximately 600 light-years away from us.

Discovered by NASA's Kepler spacecraft in 2011, Kepler-22b was one of the earliest exoplanets found within the "habitable zone" of its star, the region where conditions could theoretically allow the existence of liquid water - a key ingredient for life as we know it. The planet orbits its star in 290 days, similar to Earth's 365-day year.

However, don't start packing your bags just yet. While the planet's location and size might make it seem Earth-like, scientists are still uncertain about Kepler-22b's actual composition and atmospheric conditions. It could be a water world, an ocean-covered rocky planet, or even a gaseous mini-Neptune.

Kepler-22b encapsulates the allure of exoplanet research: the opportunity to explore strange new worlds, shedding light on the possibilities beyond our own solar system. For now, Kepler-22b remains a tantalizing mystery, a beacon in our quest to understand the universe's diverse planetary landscapes.

Fact 87 - White Dwarf: The Crystal Ball of the Universe

Astronomers refer to white dwarfs as the crystal balls of the universe, and for good reason. These dense, dying stars, remnants of the stellar life cycle, hold essential information about the past, present, and future of the cosmos. They're like celestial time capsules, patiently waiting for us to unlock their secrets.

White dwarfs are what medium-sized stars like our Sun become after exhausting their nuclear fuel. They shrink down to roughly Earth-sized objects, composed mainly of carbon and oxygen atoms squeezed together in a dense, crystalline lattice, almost like a gigantic diamond. Their surfaces are white-hot, hence the name.

In the billions of years after their formation, white dwarfs cool and fade away slowly, eventually turning into black dwarfs. However, the universe isn't old enough for any black dwarf to have formed yet. This means every white dwarf we observe is a window into the past, showing us the life cycle of stars that have long since perished.

By studying these crystalline spheres, we gain a deeper understanding of stellar evolution, the ages of galactic structures, and perhaps the destiny of our own Sun. White dwarfs, therefore, indeed act as cosmic crystal balls, revealing the universe's past and future.

Fact 88 - Earth's Doppelganger: The Venus Enigma

Venus, Earth's celestial neighbor, often referred to as our planet's 'evil twin' or 'doppelganger,' presents a profound enigma for scientists. At first glance, you might think it's a sibling of Earth. Roughly the same size and composed of similar materials, Venus sits just one planet closer to the Sun in our solar system's celestial lineup.

However, beyond these superficial resemblances, Venus is vastly different. It has a dense, choking atmosphere composed mainly of carbon dioxide, with temperatures reaching a searing 465 degrees Celsius, hot enough to melt lead. This scorching climate, coupled with an atmospheric pressure 92 times that of Earth, makes Venus the most inhospitable of the planets in our solar system.

Another intriguing factor is Venus's peculiar rotation. Unlike Earth and most other planets, Venus rotates from east to west. Even more strangely, its rotation is incredibly slow, making a Venusian day longer than a Venusian year.

Despite its hostile conditions, Venus offers a stark lesson about the potential dangers of runaway greenhouse effects. By understanding our sinister twin, we not only learn about different planetary environments, but we also gain insights into the potential future of our own planet if we fail to protect it.

Fact 89 - Shrinking Giant: The Diminishing Storm on Jupiter

One of the most prominent features on Jupiter, our solar system's largest planet, is the Great Red Spot. As you gaze at Jupiter's cloud tops, you will notice this persistent, tempestuous storm. It's a larger-than-Earth hurricane that has been furiously swirling for centuries.

The Great Red Spot was first observed in the 17th century and was estimated to be about three times the size of Earth. However, this gigantic storm isn't the unchanging feature you might imagine. Recent observations have revealed a fascinating fact: Jupiter's signature spot is gradually shrinking.

According to NASA's Voyager data from the late 1970s to more recent data from Hubble Space Telescope and Juno spacecraft, the spot has been reducing in size over the decades. Currently, it's approximately 1.3 times the size of Earth, considerably smaller than its size centuries ago.

Although scientists are not entirely sure why the storm is diminishing, some hypotheses include changes in Jupiter's climate, increased storm activity, or even collisions with smaller vortices. As the Great Red Spot continues to shrink, it offers an intriguing window into the complex atmospheric dynamics of gas giant planets.

Fact 90 - The Fast and the Curious: The Space Race History

In the midst of the Cold War, the United States and the Soviet Union entered into a competition that had more to do with scientific advancement than with military might. This contest was the Space Race, a period you may recall was marked by intense efforts to explore the final frontier.

The Space Race officially commenced with the launch of Sputnik 1 by the Soviet Union in 1957, the first artificial satellite to orbit Earth. This moment sent shockwaves around the globe, igniting a fierce competition to achieve space 'firsts'. The Soviets initially led the race, with Yuri Gagarin becoming the first man in space in 1961.

However, the United States soon caught up. The Apollo program, developed by NASA, set a bold goal to land a man on the moon. In 1969, this goal was realized when Neil Armstrong took "one small step for man, one giant leap for mankind," marking a monumental achievement in human history.

Although the Space Race concluded with the Apollo-Soyuz Test Project in 1975, the legacy of this era continues to influence space exploration today, shaping our ongoing curiosity and ambition to understand the cosmos.

Fact 91 - Shining Bright: The Luminosity of Supernovae

In the cosmic theater, few events can match the dramatic splendor of a supernova. It's the explosive death of a star, releasing a burst of light so bright, you, the spectator on Earth, can often see it with the naked eye, even from millions of light-years away.

Supernovae occur when a star, having exhausted its nuclear fuel, can no longer sustain its own gravity. The ensuing implosion and subsequent explosion results in a brilliant flash of light that can momentarily outshine an entire galaxy. This immense luminosity is driven by the release of a staggering amount of energy.

But it's not just the light show that astounds. The brightness of supernovae provides invaluable insights into cosmic distances. Astronomers use a particular kind of supernova, Type Ia, as 'standard candles'. They have a uniform brightness, so by measuring their apparent brightness from Earth, astronomers can calculate their distance. This has helped to map the universe in unprecedented detail.

So, the next time you gaze at the stars, remember that their serene glow belies an immensely powerful and bright future. In the world of astronomy, even the death of a star brings light to the darkness.

Fact 92 - Cosmic Tsunami: The Energy Waves in Galaxies

The cosmos is a bustling, energetic place, and one of its most spectacular displays of energy comes in the form of waves rippling through galaxies, akin to tsunamis on Earth. However, instead of water, these cosmic tsunamis are made up of hot gas and energetic particles, creating spectacular arcs and tendrils that span hundreds of thousands of light-years.

These "tsunamis" are caused by supermassive black holes at the center of galaxies. As material spirals into the black hole, it heats up, releasing enormous amounts of energy into the surrounding galaxy. This energy forms vast waves that ripple outwards, a phenomenon known as "galactic winds".

These galactic winds have a significant impact on the evolution of galaxies. They can compress gas in their path, triggering the birth of new stars. However, they can also blow gas and dust out of the galaxy, which can suppress star formation and change the galaxy's shape over time.

In the end, cosmic tsunamis are one of the many awe-inspiring, yet disruptive phenomena in our universe. Even as you read this, they are shaping the galaxies, turning the cosmos into a dynamic, ever-changing sea of stars.

Fact 93 - The International Space Station

Orbiting Earth every 90 minutes, the International Space Station (ISS) is a marvel of human engineering and international cooperation. This spaceport, which has been continuously occupied since November 2000, serves as a home, research facility, and stage for astronauts from around the globe.

Roughly the size of a football field, the ISS is the largest structure humans have ever put into space. It is a joint project between NASA, Roscosmos, ESA, JAXA, and CSA, showing the powerful collaboration possible when nations unite in the pursuit of knowledge and exploration.

The ISS is a hub of scientific research, with astronauts conducting experiments that can only be done in the unique microgravity environment of space. This research spans a wide range of fields, from human biology to astronomy, providing valuable insights that benefit people on Earth and guide future space missions.

So, as you go about your day, remember that over your head, astronauts are living and working in space, carrying out important research and pushing the boundaries of our knowledge and capabilities in the vast cosmic frontier.

Fact 94 - Space Spaghetti: The Theory of Spaghettification

Picture this: you're falling into a black hole, your body stretching and thinning into a long, noodle-like shape. This isn't a surreal dream, but the phenomenon known as 'spaghettification', a terrifying yet fascinating concept in the realm of theoretical physics.

Spaghettification is the vertical stretching and horizontal compression that happens to objects when they get too close to a black hole due to the immense gravitational forces at play. The term was humorously coined by physicist Stephen Hawking, as the effect resembles turning an object into a thin string of spaghetti.

The process is due to what's known as a tidal force, which is a difference in gravitational pull on different parts of an object. The side of you closer to the black hole would feel a stronger pull than the side farther away, resulting in a powerful stretching effect.

Although the chances of you personally experiencing spaghettification are extremely low, the concept provides a stark illustration of the extreme and often mind-bending consequences of the powerful forces at play in our universe.

Fact 95 - Runaway Universe: The Mystery of Dark Energy

Imagine a force so powerful and elusive that it's accelerating the expansion of the universe itself. This isn't a scene from a science fiction novel, but a real-life mystery scientists are grappling with today. They call this enigmatic force 'Dark Energy'.

Dark Energy is an unknown form of energy that is theorized to permeate all of space. It's thought to be the driving force behind the accelerating expansion of the universe, a discovery that earned the 2011 Nobel Prize in Physics. Yet, despite its significant implications, dark energy remains shrouded in mystery.

Astrophysicists have few clues about what dark energy actually is. Some propose it's a property of space itself, represented by the cosmological constant in Einstein's field equations of general relativity. Others suggest it's a new, undiscovered particle or the result of modifying the laws of gravity at large scales.

Whatever the true nature of dark energy, its discovery has shaken the foundations of cosmology. It's a prime example of how, even in the vastness of the universe, there are still secrets waiting to be unraveled, and dark energy is perhaps one of the most intriguing of them all.

Fact 96 - The James Webb Space Telescope

As an avid sky gazer, you may know about the Hubble Space Telescope. Now, let's introduce its successor, the James Webb Space Telescope (JWST), which has been touted as the biggest leap in astronomy since Galileo's telescope.

The JWST is a space telescope developed by NASA, ESA, and the Canadian Space Agency. It boasts a mirror more than twice the size of Hubble's, offering unprecedented resolution and sensitivity. It's primarily designed to observe the universe in infrared, enabling it to peer through cosmic dust and gaze at the earliest stars and galaxies.

What sets the JWST apart is its ability to look back over 13.5 billion years, to see the first light after the Big Bang. It's expected to revolutionize our understanding of how galaxies evolve and to provide new insights into the formation of stars and planets. It may even be able to detect signs of life on exoplanets.

So, the next time you look up at the stars, remember the James Webb Space Telescope, the most powerful space observatory ever built. It's a cosmic detective that's on a mission to solve some of the universe's biggest mysteries.

Fact 97 - The Space Sculptor: The Impact of Solar Wind

You may have heard about the winds on Earth, but have you ever wondered about winds in space? Welcome to the world of solar wind, a constant stream of charged particles released from the Sun's atmosphere that has a profound impact on our solar system.

Solar wind is composed mostly of electrons, protons, and alpha particles, moving at an average speed of about 400 km per second. This cosmic wind has the power to shape and change objects in space, much like how earthly winds can carve and mold the landscape.

This solar outflow can have significant effects on Earth's magnetosphere, causing beautiful phenomena like the Northern and Southern Lights. However, it's also a significant challenge for space missions and satellites as the charged particles can interfere with electronic systems and cause damage.

So the next time you think of wind, remember it's not just an earthly phenomenon. The solar wind, a space sculptor, shapes our cosmic neighborhood, creating captivating phenomena and posing significant challenges for our journey into space.

Fact 98 - The Smallest Star: Meet EBLM J0555-57Ab

When you gaze at the night sky, do you ever wonder about the diversity of the stars? They vary enormously in size, from giants hundreds of times the size of our sun to the smallest known star, EBLM J0555-57Ab.

EBLM J0555-57Ab is an astonishing celestial object that barely made the cut to be classified as a star. Its diameter is nearly 80,000 kilometers, just a bit larger than Jupiter, making it the smallest star discovered so far. However, despite its size, it has 85 times the mass of Jupiter.

This tiny titan's size is a testament to the incredible diversity of the universe. Its small size and mass bring it close to the dividing line between stars and brown dwarfs - 'failed' stars that didn't have enough mass to ignite nuclear fusion.

So remember, even in the vast universe, small wonders like EBLM J0555-57Ab exist. These tiny stars stretch our understanding of celestial bodies and remind us that, in the cosmos, size doesn't always dictate significance.

Fact 99 - A Song of Ice and Cosmic Dust

Do you appreciate the cosmic ballet of planets and their rings? If so, you'll find the rings of Uranus fascinating. They are a cosmic composition of ice and dust, singing a unique song in the celestial symphony.

These elegant rings, thirteen in total, were discovered relatively recently in 1977. Unlike the flamboyantly displayed rings of Saturn, Uranus's rings are narrow, dark, and enigmatic, composed primarily of large particles and boulders of water ice and radiation-altered substances.

What makes them so unique is their sheer darkness. The rings reflect only a tiny portion of the sunlight that falls upon them. This characteristic, coupled with their narrow width, makes them almost stealthy in the grand scheme of the solar system.

So, the next time you ponder the cosmos, remember Uranus's rings - a graceful composition of ice and cosmic dust, quietly performing their celestial ballet. These rings, subtle and understated, bring a special kind of charm to our understanding of the planets and the intricate harmony that prevails in our universe.

Fact 100 - The Stellar Zoo: The Various Types of Galaxies

You might think that galaxies are all the same, but that's far from the truth. Just as Earth has diverse ecosystems filled with a wide range of creatures, the universe too hosts a myriad of galaxies, each with their own unique characteristics and forms. Welcome to the stellar zoo!

The most commonly known type is the spiral galaxy, like our Milky Way. These galaxies feature beautiful, sprawling arms spiraling out from a dense core. Imagine an astronomical pinwheel twirling in the cosmic wind, and you have an idea of a spiral galaxy's majestic presence.

Another type is the elliptical galaxy. These giants of the universe are spherical or elongated, often appearing like giant blobs of starlight. They lack the defined structure of spiral galaxies, yet their massive size and luminosity make them some of the most awe-inspiring objects in the cosmos.

Finally, there are irregular galaxies, the wild cards of the cosmic deck. These galaxies don't fit into the typical categories, possessing an unusual, often chaotic structure that defies simple classification. As you can see, the universe is home to a diverse stellar zoo, where galaxies of all shapes and sizes add to the grandeur of the cosmos.

Conclusion

And so, dear reader, we reach the end of this celestial journey. 1000 facts later, we hope that your mind is as full as the night sky is with stars. From the birth of a star to the death of a galaxy, from the discovery of distant exoplanets to the mysteries of black holes and dark energy, "1000 Amazing Facts about Space" has guided you across the universe, illuminating the most captivating aspects of our infinite cosmos.

But remember, as vast as our journey has been, we have only just begun to explore the boundless expanse that is space. We've merely skimmed the surface of the mysteries it holds. Each fact, each page, each chapter in this book is but a small fragment of the larger, ever-expanding universe of knowledge that awaits us.

Space exploration continues to push forward, its pace quickened by advances in technology and our relentless curiosity. New spacecraft are venturing further into the unknown, new telescopes are peering deeper into the cosmos, and new discoveries are made almost daily. As we move forward, the universe only seems to become more mysterious, more awe-inspiring, and more beautiful.

We hope that "1000 Amazing Facts about Space" has sparked your curiosity, stirred your imagination, and inspired you to look up at the night sky with a newfound sense of wonder. Always remember: in the realm of the cosmos, the more we learn, the more there is yet to discover. Until our paths cross again in another constellation of knowledge, we leave you with this – continue to explore, continue to dream, and continue to marvel at the amazing universe that surrounds us. The cosmos awaits, dear reader, so let's keep reaching for the stars!

Quizz

1) What is the theorized cause of Earth's moon formation?

    a) Direct collision with another planet
    b) The Big Whack Theory
    c) Accretion from space debris
    d) It's always been there

2) Which of the following is not a type of galaxy?

    a) Spiral
    b) Elliptical
    c) Square
    d) Irregular

3) What is a unique feature of the exoplanet Kepler-22b?

    a) It's completely covered in ice
    b) It's a giant planet compared to Earth
    c) It has a square orbit
    d) It's smaller than Earth

4) Which space telescope is often called the 'Cosmic Detective'?

    a) Spitzer Space Telescope
    b) James Webb Space Telescope
    c) Hubble Space Telescope
    d) Kepler Space Telescope

5) What is the tallest mountain in the solar system?

    a) Mount Everest
    b) Mauna Kea
    c) Mount Kilimanjaro
    d) Olympus Mons on Mars

6) What is the Rogue Planet?

    a) A planet that orbits two suns
    b) A planet that has escaped its original star and
       wanders the cosmos
    c) The coldest known planet in the universe
    d) The most distant planet in our solar system

7) What is the theory of Spaghettification related to?

    a) The formation of galaxies
    b) The process one would theoretically experience
       falling into a black hole
    c) The expansion of the universe
    d) The formation of stars

8) What's special about EBLM J0555-57Ab?

    a) It's the largest star discovered
    b) It's the smallest star discovered
    c) It's a rogue star, wandering without a galaxy
    d) It's the hottest star known

9) What is the Andromeda Galaxy known for?

    a) Being the smallest galaxy
    b) Being our Milky Way's twin
    c) Its unique spiral structure
    d) Being the furthest galaxy from us

10) What is the primary purpose of the Asteroid Belt in our Solar System?

    a) To provide a shield for the inner planets from meteor impacts
    b) To act as a source of precious metals for future space mining
    c) To serve as a ring for the solar system
    d) It has no specific purpose

11) What is the theory behind the Nemesis Star?

    a) It's a second sun in our solar system
    b) It's the cause of Earth's moon formation
    c) It's a theoretical companion star to our sun that could cause mass extinctions
    d) It's a star destined to collide with our sun

12) What is unique about the Northern Lights?

    a) They are a result of solar winds interacting with Earth's magnetic field
    b) They are unique to the North Pole
    c) They only occur during the summer solstice

d) They are the reflections of Earth's city lights on the atmosphere

13) What is unique about Jupiter's moon Europa?

a) It has an active volcano
b) It has the tallest mountain in the solar system
c) It's believed to have a subsurface ocean, making it a potential home for life
d) It's the largest moon in the solar system

14) What celestial event happens when the Moon comes between Earth and the Sun?

a) Lunar Eclipse
b) Solar Eclipse
c) The Blue Moon
d) The Super Moon

15) What is the main reason for the existence of Saturn's rings?

a) They are made from an exploded moon
b) They are remnants from Saturn's formation
c) They are composed of ice from comets
d) They are a result of Saturn's strong magnetic field

16) Which is the richest asteroid known in the Universe?

a) Vesta

b) Eros
c) Pallas
d) Psyche

17) What is the primary effect of a Solar Flare?

a) Causes a change in Earth's magnetic field
b) Can disrupt communication systems on Earth
c) Creates a hole in the ozone layer
d) Causes an increase in Earth's global temperature

18) What do Pulsars primarily emit?

a) Gamma rays
b) X-rays
c) Radio waves
d) Visible light

19) What's special about the weather on Neptune?

a) It's the hottest planet in our solar system
b) It rains diamonds
c) It has the calmest weather in the solar system
d) It has the strongest winds in the solar system

20) What is Voyager 1 known for?

a) The first spacecraft to land on Mars
b) The spacecraft that discovered the Oort Cloud
c) The first human-made object to enter interstellar space
d) The spacecraft that discovered water on the moon

Answers

1) What is the theorized cause of Earth's moon formation?

Correct answer: b)The Big Whack Theory

2) Which of the following is not a type of galaxy?

Correct answer: c)Square

3) What is a unique feature of the exoplanet Kepler-22b?

Correct answer: b)It's a giant planet compared to Earth

4) Which space telescope is often called the 'Cosmic Detective'?

Correct answer: b)James Webb Space Telescope

5) What is the tallest mountain in the solar system?

Correct answer: d)Olympus Mons on Mars

6) What is the Rogue Planet?

Correct answer: b)A planet that has escaped its original star and wanders the cosmos

7) What is the theory of Spaghettification related to?

Correct answer: b)The process one would theoretically experience falling into a black hole

8) What's special about EBLM J0555-57Ab?

Correct answer: b)It's the smallest star discovered

9) What is the Andromeda Galaxy known for?

Correct answer: c)Its unique spiral structure

10) What is the primary purpose of the Asteroid Belt in our Solar System?

Correct answer: a)To provide a shield for the inner planets from meteor impacts

11) What is the theory behind the Nemesis Star?

Correct answer: c)It's a theoretical companion star to our sun that could cause mass extinctions

12) What is unique about the Northern Lights?

Correct answer: a)They are a result of solar winds interacting with Earth's magnetic field

13) What is unique about Jupiter's moon Europa?

Correct answer: c)It's believed to have a subsurface ocean, making it a potential home for life

14) What celestial event happens when the Moon comes between Earth and the Sun?

Correct answer: b)Solar Eclipse

15) What is the main reason for the existence of Saturn's rings?

Correct answer: b)They are remnants from Saturn's formation

16) Which is the richest asteroid known in the Universe?

Correct answer: d)Psyche

17) What is the primary effect of a Solar Flare?

Correct answer: b)Can disrupt communication systems on Earth

18) What do Pulsars primarily emit?

Correct answer: c)Radio waves

19) What's special about the weather on Neptune?

Correct answer: b)It rains diamonds

20) What is Voyager 1 known for?

Correct answer: c)The first human-made object to enter interstellar space

Printed in Great Britain
by Amazon

34745608R10068